LINGUISTIC SURVEYS OF AFRICA

Volume 16

THE BANTU LANGUAGES OF WESTERN EQUATORIAL AFRICA

THE BANTU LANGUAGES OF WESTERN EQUATORIAL AFRICA
Handbook of African Languages

MALCOLM GUTHRIE

LONDON AND NEW YORK

First published in 1953 by Oxford University Press

This edition first published in 2018
by Routledge
2 Park Square, Milton Park, Abingdon, Oxon OX14 4RN

and by Routledge
711 Third Avenue, New York, NY 10017

Routledge is an imprint of the Taylor & Francis Group, an informa business

© 1953 International African Institute

All rights reserved. No part of this book may be reprinted or reproduced or utilised in any form or by any electronic, mechanical, or other means, now known or hereafter invented, including photocopying and recording, or in any information storage or retrieval system, without permission in writing from the publishers.

Trademark notice: Product or corporate names may be trademarks or registered trademarks, and are used only for identification and explanation without intent to infringe.

British Library Cataloguing in Publication Data
A catalogue record for this book is available from the British Library

ISBN: 978-1-138-08975-4 (Set)
ISBN: 978-1-315-10381-5 (Set) (ebk)
ISBN: 978-1-138-09682-0 (Volume 16) (hbk)
ISBN: 978-1-138-09708-7 (Volume 16) (pbk)
ISBN: 978-1-315-10509-3 (Volume 16) (ebk)

Publisher's Note
The publisher has gone to great lengths to ensure the quality of this reprint but points out that some imperfections in the original copies may be apparent.

Disclaimer
The publisher has made every effort to trace copyright holders and would welcome correspondence from those they have been unable to trace.

Due to modern production methods, it has not been possible to reproduce the fold-out maps within the book. Please visit www.routledge.com to view them.

THE
BANTU LANGUAGES
OF WESTERN
EQUATORIAL AFRICA

By
MALCOLM GUTHRIE

Published for the
INTERNATIONAL AFRICAN INSTITUTE
by the
OXFORD UNIVERSITY PRESS
LONDON NEW YORK TORONTO
1953

Oxford University Press, Amen House, London E.C.4
GLASGOW NEW YORK TORONTO MELBOURNE WELLINGTON
BOMBAY CALCUTTA MADRAS KARACHI CAPE TOWN IBADAN
Geoffrey Cumberlege, Publisher to the University

This study has been prepared and published in connexion with the Handbook of African Languages and with the aid of a grant from the British Colonial Development and Welfare Fund.

PRINTED IN GREAT BRITAIN
AT THE UNIVERSITY PRESS, OXFORD
BY CHARLES BATEY, PRINTER TO THE UNIVERSITY

CONTENTS

INTRODUCTION	5
METHOD OF DESCRIBING LINGUISTIC FEATURES	9
A.10 LUNDU-MBO GROUP	15
A.20 DUALA GROUP	20
A.30 BUBE-BENGA GROUP	24
A.40 BASA GROUP	28
A.50 BAFIA GROUP	33
A.60 SANAGA GROUP	36
A.70 YAUNDE-FANG GROUP	40
A.80 MAKAA-NJEM GROUP	45
A.90 KAKA GROUP	50
B.10 MYENE CLUSTER	55
B.20 KELE GROUP	59
B.30 TSOGO GROUP	64
B.40 SHIRA-PUNU GROUP	67
B.50 NJABI GROUP	70
B.60 MBETE GROUP	74
B.70 TEKE GROUP	77
B.80 TENDE-YANZI GROUP	81
C.10 NGUNDI GROUP	85
C.20 MBOSHI GROUP	88
INDEX OF LANGUAGES	93
MAP OF BANTU LANGUAGES OF WESTERN EQUATORIAL AFRICA	*Inside Back Cover*

INTRODUCTION

THE area covered by this work is one that has long been recognized as presenting many problems from the point of view of Bantu linguistic studies. In my *Classification of the Bantu Languages* it was pointed out that the languages of Zones A and B were those about which there was least reliable information. There had been a number of scattered studies of some of the languages, but most of these either were written during the last century or were confined to one or two important languages. A certain amount had been written on the distribution of individual tribes and groups of tribes by German and French writers. Most notable among these is G. Tessmann, whose ethnic map of Cameroun has long been the main authority for this area. G. Bruel in his work on L'Afrique Equatoriale Française gave a map and some information on the tribes of Gabon, Moyen Congo, and Oubangui-Chari, but this was entirely ethnographic and his linguistic statements were very fragmentary and scarcely authoritative.

Arising out of this state of affairs I took the opportunity provided in 1949 by the authorities of the School of Oriental and African Studies; University of London, to make a special research trip throughout the area concerned. This was undertaken with the willing co-operation of the Office de la Recherche Scientifique de la France d'Outre-Mer and of the Institut pour la Recherche Scientifique en Afrique Central in Brussels. This resulted in my receiving the goodwill and active assistance of the French and Belgian authorities throughout the whole of my journey, a fact that enabled the available time to be used to the greatest advantage. During the course of this visit many languages were investigated, and where it proved useful recordings were taken. As a result almost all the material set out in this present work is based on the notes taken in the field, and in many cases presents completely new facts.

The sources of the information used are listed at the end of the linguistic description of each of the groups of languages dealt with. Where my own material has been served as a source this is indicated by referring to 'MS. notes'. Other useful works that throw some light upon the languages concerned are also mentioned, including one or two that have not actually been consulted.

At the same time as the researches on which this present work is based were being undertaken, the International African Institute's survey of the northern limit of the Bantu languages was in progress. In some cases the report of this Northern Bantu Borderline Survey (NBBS) contains information that supplements that to be found in these linguistic outlines. Since however the intention of the two books is different, this has been written in such a way that it is complete in itself. Nevertheless, those who are particularly interested in the fascinating languages of this area should consult the NBBS for further details on the languages on or near the actual Bantu border.

TRANSCRIPTION

In a work dealing with many languages of this kind, the problem of transcription is a serious one. The main principles followed are the use of the I.P.A. system with one or two minor modifications that are explained in the following paragraphs.

(a) The use of **y** as the semi-vowel corresponding to **i** instead of **j**. The character **ü** is then used for the sound represented by **y** in the I.P.A. spelling.

(b) Peripheral vowels are spelt with eleven different symbols in which cedillas are used under **i** and **u** to indicate a very close articulation, the unmarked vowels then being available for a more lax variety. A close **e** (or **o**) is spelt with a dot underneath to distinguish it from a mid variety such as occurs in five-vowel languages; this latter is then written with the plain roman letter. The open vowel characters **ɛ** and **ɔ** are used only for the more open qualities of vowel found in many seven-vowel languages.

Centralized vowels are spelt with the usual diaeresis, except that **ɨ** and **ʉ** are used for a centralized variety of **į** and **ų** respectively, **ï** then being available for a high central vowel.

(c) In order to economize in the use of symbols, special characters are not used to represent implosive voiced stops, it being noted in each case whether the consonants involved are implosive or not. Similarly in at least one language **ɨ** is regularly spelt **i**, since the plain character is not required there for any other sound.

(d) Since the distinction between a palatal nasal consonant and **ny** is not operative in any of the examples quoted, the digraph is used throughout, instead of the special character **ɲ**.

(e) Special diacritics have to be used in some places, but these are explained wherever the need for them arises. Where tones are marked, a two-tone system only is required, so the higher level is marked by an acute accent, the lower level being indicated by the absence of an accent. A circumflex accent is used for a falling tone, and an inverted circumflex for a rising tone. Where a final syllabic nasal with the lower level of tone occurs after a vowel with a high tone, this fact is shown by the use of a grave accent on the nasal.

Nomenclature

(a) *Names of Languages.* Wherever possible the name given for a language is that used by the people themselves, and this is written in a phonetic transcription. The only departures from the usual spelling are that **dj**, **c**, **ḇ**, and **g̱** are written instead of **dʒ**, **tʃ**, **β**, and **ɣ** respectively, because of the difficulty of using capital forms of **ʒ**, **ʃ**, **β** and **ɣ**.

The usual method of giving the names of Bantu languages has been followed. This involves the omission of any prefix used to denote language, the prefix then being given after the language name in the list. In many cases among these languages there is no such prefix, and sometimes it will be noted that the word given actually looks like the name of the people. It has always been verified, however, that this is what is used by the speakers of a language when referring to it in an actual sentence in the language itself. Other names that have been used which may in many cases be better known are noted in square brackets.

The names given to the groups are for convenience of reference only, and for these a more common even if less accurate spelling may be used.

(b) *Place Names.* These are given according to the official spelling used in the country concerned. Thus, for example, there will be found the French spelling Cameroun for the territory under French mandate, the English spelling Cameroon for the mountain, and Cameroons for the territory under British mandate.

INTRODUCTION

CLASSIFICATION AND INDEX NUMBERS

Those who are acquainted with the system of classification adopted in my previous work on this subject will recognize that there is a fundamental modification in the arrangement of Zones A and B. In effect the classification for these two zones set out in this present work entirely supersedes the tentative one previously suggested. Since the same principles have been followed as in the earlier work, and the differences are merely due to more complete and reliable data, this revised classification for Zones A and B can be integrated into the remainder of the complete one previously developed.

In the case of Zone C it will be observed that two groups only have been described. Of these C.10 is the revised form of the corresponding group in the original classification. The other group C.20 however is completely new, since these languages were not previously known to exist. The introduction of this group involves a small modification of the original index numbers of Zone C. As a result of this, the original groups C.30 and C.40 form one continuous group C.41–45, while the original group C.20 is now numbered C.30.

THE MAP

In compiling a linguistic map of part of central Africa on a fairly large scale certain problems are inevitably encountered. The chief difficulty is that such a map might easily give a wrong impression of the importance of some of the languages, since unless the population figures are borne in mind the area over which the language is spoken may not be of much significance. A further point is that in many cases there are relatively large tracts of uninhabited country between the roads and tracks along which the speakers of a language happen to live. Where possible, as in the case of A.84 for example, the boundaries of the language have been made to conform approximately to the actual area where the speakers live. In other cases, such as B.25, it is known that not all the area enclosed by the boundary of the main region where the language is spoken is inhabited, but it was not feasible to break up the area into small groups, since the population is fairly well scattered throughout it.

The net result is that where a large unbroken area is shown it must not be assumed that it is uniformly populated. Where areas have been shown stippled with no language marked it is reasonably certain that these have either no inhabitants or only pygmies, who in this part of Africa speak a non-Bantu language of their own.

In order to give the map some depth, the names and index numbers of adjacent Bantu languages in other groups have been shown. Where no index-number is given and the language name is in parentheses, this is because it is not Bantu and has only been inserted in order to make clear that the area concerned is not uninhabited.

The information contained on the map is based on the most reliable data obtainable, and in the majority of cases was verified locally. In particular special acknowledgement is due to the most useful *Inventaire Ethnique du Sud-Cameroun* by Mme Dugast, for the languages of the southern part of Cameroun.

METHOD OF DESCRIBING LINGUISTIC FEATURES

SINCE there are so many languages to be dealt with it would be impracticable to give even an outline of the main features of each of them. To keep the work within limits an outline is given of the main characteristics of each group separately. To do this one language is used as the type for each group, for the purpose of listing examples of the nominal prefixes, verbal conjugation, and personal prefixes. Other features are illustrated from whichever language is the most suitable.

In choosing the features to be dealt with in these descriptions regard has had to be had to those things which are of general interest for Bantu language studies as well as to those characteristics which have formed the basis of the linguistic classification set out in this work. The conceptual system of grammatical description is for all practical purposes identical with that implied in my *Classification of the Bantu Languages*, and some of the more important aspects of it will be clear from the following notes explaining the framework used to outline the characteristics of each group.

Since the description in each case of necessity derives from the nature of the individual languages involved, not all the subdivisions of the following headings will appear for each group. Indeed it may happen that a main heading is not required in a given case, although negative statements are sometimes included, since they may be important for classificatory purposes. For example, if one particular language only were being described, it would be out of place to state that it had no special object substitutes, but in a work covering many different languages even the absence of such a category may be important enough to be noted.

The following then is the general scheme of the outline followed for each group.

A. SOUND PATTERNS

Under this heading there are considered several different aspects of the sounds, both individual and in combination.

1. Kinds of Syllables

There is a wide divergence from language to language in the kinds of syllables that occur. Without attempting to give a close definition of the term 'syllable', it is mainly used to refer to any fragment of a sentence which is, or can be, uttered on a distinct level of tone. Some languages are notable for the fact that many of the items used consist of one syllable only. A further fact which has to be noted is whether or not a given language makes use of closed syllables, i.e. those in which the final sound is a consonant and not a vowel. In some languages there are syllables that contain no vowel at all, more especially those that consist of nasal consonants in final position. Here again it is useful to note even the absence of such a feature in certain cases.

2. Vowel Series

The next feature to be noted is the kind of vowel series that occur in 'radical position', that is in the first syllable of stems and radicals. It has to be stated how many distinctions of vowel quality occur here, and whether or not there is a distinction of vowel quantity. The occurrence of centralized vowels and nasalized vowels also has to be noted.

In the case of certain languages there is an important difference between the vowel series in non-final radical position and in final position, this latter being a special case independently of the number of syllables in the stem or base.

3. *Vowel Sequences*

In a number of languages there are rules governing which vowels occur in sequence with one another. For example, it sometimes happens that there is correlation between the presence of a very close vowel in radical position, and the quality of the vowel of a prefix or suffix in sequence with it.

4. *Consonant Sounds*

It is not possible or necessary to describe in detail all the distinctions of consonant sounds that have been found to occur in any language. There are however certain things to be noted in each case, such as the occurrence of imploded voiced stops, the use of fricative sounds, or the presence of consonants with double articulation.

5. *Tone Patterns*

Wherever it is feasible the tones of all the examples are indicated, since for the most part to omit the tones means that a word or sentence cannot be properly identified. In some cases this cannot be done because there is no tone pattern that is always characteristic of a given word, mainly because the actual pattern used in any given case is determined by syntactical relationships.

One feature which is very important in some languages is what is termed 'tone-slip'. This refers to the behaviour of adjacent 'high-tones' in those cases in which the second of two high-tones is pronounced at a level distinctly lower than the first, in accordance with fixed rules. In order to avoid multiplying tone marks the incidence of tone-slip is indicated by the use of a superior exclamation mark, which also enables successive tone-slips to be shown without additional complication.

Reference is usually made, with examples, to the use of tone as the sole feature distinguishing lexical units wherever this has been observed.

B. Class System

Even the most fragmentary description of any Bantu language must contain some list of the classes that operate the system of grammatical agreement. The different kinds of agreement are distinguished by the use of numbers that correspond from language to language in accordance with the results of comparative Bantu linguistic studies. In a few cases there are uncertainties, and in particular some difficulty is encountered where distinct classes have 'fallen together'. To avoid duplication, one number only has been arbitrarily assigned in such cases, usually the lower of the two numbers involved. For example, if in a given language the agreement corresponding to Class 4 in other languages is indistinguishable from that corresponding to Class 8, the class in question is numbered 4.

The various kinds of nominal fall into two main groups, according as they belong to a series which runs through the whole of the classes or not. In the latter case, where the series is relatively short or even consists of one item only, the prefix is termed 'independent', whereas a member of a complete series of prefixes that can be used with a given stem is termed 'dependent'. It is necessary therefore to list separately the various independent prefixes found in the type language, and to make some observations about the kinds of dependent prefixes that occur.

1. *Independent Prefixes*

In order to combine the list of the classes with the pairs of classes correlated with the singular/plural distinction, the independent prefixes are grouped together in pairs wherever possible, even when this means repeating a given class that occurs as the plural member of more than one pair.

In some cases there are special shapes for independent prefixes that occur in junction with a vowel. These are noted wherever the variant is sufficiently different.

In some languages the shape of an independent prefix is different with certain stems, especially in the case of those with one syllable. Where this has been noted examples are usually given.

2. *Dependent Prefixes*

Since the purpose of the outline is to quote the principal features, it is not possible to list in detail all the different series of dependent prefixes. Under this heading therefore general observations only are given, with some examples in the case of things requiring to be particularly noted.

The behaviour of extra dependent prefixes, mainly whether they are attached with a linking vowel or not, is noted in each case.

C. Possessives

In the case of certain languages the possessive stems present certain difficulties which make it desirable to refer to them even in an outline. In those groups where there are no unusual features this section is omitted.

D. Numerals

For each group a note is made of the general system of counting underlying the numerals. In addition the grammatical behaviour of the numerals '1'–'9' is described. Apart from these characteristics further details are given only if there are any peculiarities in the numerals for the multiples of ten.

E. Nominal Sentences

In a number of cases sentences are commonly used consisting entirely of nominals. Since this also provides an opportunity to show the operation of the grammatical agreement, two such sentences are given wherever they have been found. In languages where nominal sentences have not been observed the corresponding type of sentence is given for purposes of comparison.

12   METHOD OF DESCRIBING LINGUISTIC FEATURES

F. Verbal System

Within the compass of the outlines given it is not possible to do more than to indicate the more important features of the verbal system. None of the lists of tenses that are given is necessarily exhaustive, although the number quoted for the type language does reflect the complexity of the tenses in each case.

1. *Conjugation.*

In each language the principal affirmative tenses are given first, with an approximate indication of their commonest meanings. As these notes are not intended to stand for a linguistic description, there is no objection to the use of such approximate terms as 'past' and 'future'. As is the case with many Bantu languages there are two main types of meaning expressed by means of one-word tenses. Some tenses may refer to an event in such a way as merely to indicate the relative time at which it occurs. In others, however, there may be no time reference at all, or rather the time reference is zero, i.e. it is derived entirely from the act of speech, the tense then referring to some aspect of the event described by the verbal. The three main aspects indicated in this way are Completion, Progress, and Repetition. In a few cases it is useful to show tenses which refer to an aspect of Repetition in past time. The terms 'Remote Past', 'Recent Past', and 'Immediate Past' are all relative but in each case the tense referring to more distant time always precedes the one referring to nearer time.

In almost all cases the tense sign for each tense is shown in the shape in which it most commonly occurs. It by no means follows however that with other radicals the shape of the tense sign will be exactly as quoted. The radical chosen in each case to illustrate the conjugation is one which displays the minimum of complication.

2. *Negation*

Since one of the most important features of the verbal system is concerned with negation, this has to be described in each language. In some cases there are distinct negative tenses which may have tense signs different from those of the affirmative tenses, or may be fewer in number than the affirmative tenses. In either of these cases numbered tenses of the negative conjugation are illustrated separately.

If it happens that there are no negative tenses, or if the negative tenses are characterized merely by the presence of a regular 'negative' element, then there is plainly nothing to be gained by setting out the tenses afresh. In such cases the construction of negative sentences is, however, indicated under the simple heading of negation.

3. *Personal Prefixes*

The only other verbal element which is given for each type language is the series of prefixes for each of the three persons in Classes 1 and 2. In a few cases there are certain facts about the dependent prefixes of other classes which have been noted for their special interest.

4. *Object Substitutes*

Where there are special elements or words used as object substitutes, the formation of these is noted. In other cases reference is made to this category only if there is something unusual in its behaviour.

METHOD OF DESCRIBING LINGUISTIC FEATURES

5. Relative Constructions

In some languages there are special types of relative construction which are worth noting. If the antecedent is subject of the relative clause, this fact is denoted by the use of the term 'subject antecedent'. Similarly the term 'object antecedent' refers to the other type of relative construction.

G. NOMINO-VERBALS

Another distinctive feature of groups of languages is the formation of nomino-verbals, more especially with respect to the class of the nominal prefix. This is therefore noted in the case of each group.

H. EXTENSIONS

In the languages of this area there is a wide divergence in the regularity of the occurrence of extended radicals. For this reason there will be found some information under this heading in each case, even though it may be merely negative or fragmentary. For the sake of brevity well-known terms such as 'Applied' and 'Causative' are used to refer to the various types of extension.

K. ADDITIONAL OBSERVATIONS

After the outline of the main linguistic features of the group, there is a section consisting of information of a more general nature about the languages of the group.

1. Vocabulary Content

It would have been desirable to attempt to assess the closeness of relationship between the vocabularies of languages in different groups. To do this, however, would have involved the compiling of reasonably complete word-lists for those of the type languages for which no such information had been previously obtained. Since this was impracticable, only the most general statements about the relationships of the vocabularies can be made.

Under this heading then will be found notes about the occurrence of items common to the group that are also peculiar to it. In addition some comment is made on the relationship of the vocabularies of the group to those of languages elsewhere in Bantu Africa.

2. Sound Correspondences

In an exhaustive work it would have been necessary to deal in detail with the question of the correspondences in the sounds of related items between the languages of the area and the rest of the Bantu family. To describe these 'sound-shifts' would have involved making use of the whole range of comparative Bantu linguistics, which plainly would be outside the scope of this work. Instead, use is made of the 'starred forms' developed in recent studies in this field, which are to be set out in a forthcoming work on this subject. This means that a concise method of representing the sound correspondences is available, although the full implications of the method cannot be explained here. In effect the use of the following type of equations is that not only in these three languages, but in any others where a similar starred radical is applicable, there is a regular correspondence between the sounds involved, A.24 *-túŋg- → -lóŋg- 'build'; A.43a *-túŋg- → -ɔŋ- 'build'; A.83 *-túŋg- → -tụụ 'build'. The same thing holds good where single sounds are selected for similar treatment.

3. Internal Relationships

From the description of the linguistic features, it will be clear that in some groups there is a difference in complexity of structure from language to language. Without going into a detailed discussion of all the issues involved, some indication will be given under this heading about the relative complexity of the members of a group. Thus for example in A.81 there are mainly dissyllabic stems while in others in the group, such as A.84, there are mainly monosyllabic stems, which could have been produced by the disintegration of dissyllabic stems comparable to those in A.81. This state of affairs will be described by saying that there is a reduction in complexity from A.81 to A.84. The indication of such a reduction does not imply that there has been a process of disintegration from the one language to the other, but is merely a statement of their relationship.

4. General Affinities

For each of the groups it is useful to give a brief statement about the affinities of the languages to those of adjacent groups. In addition any notable linguistic proximity to other languages in the Bantu field that has been noted will be indicated.

A.10 LUNDU-MBO GROUP

A.11 *LUNDU* Cluster
These dialects are spoken in British Cameroons, mainly on the western side between Mamfe and the coast.
A.11a *LUNDU* [Balundu]
A.11b *ƉGƆRƆ* [Ngolo]
A.11c *BAKŲNDŲ*
A.11d *BATAƉGA* and *BĮMA*
A.11e *EKŲMBƐ* and *MBƆƉGƐ*

A.12 *BARŲƐ* [Lue, W. Kundu]
Spoken behind the coastal belt in the central area of British Cameroons.

A.13 *BALQƉ*
Spoken on both sides of the boundary between British Cameroons and Cameroun, to the south and west of Mbanga.

A.14 *BƆƉKẸƉ*
Spoken just to the north of Mbanga in Cameroun, along the boundary with British Cameroons.

A.15 *MBO* Cluster
These dialects are spoken on both sides of the boundary between British Cameroons and Cameroun around and to the west of Dschang and N'Kongsomba.
A.15a *BAFƆ*
A.15b *KƆƆSə*, a- [Nkosi]
Spoken also by the Mwamenam.
A.15c *SWASə*, n- [Basosi]
A.15d *LƆƉ*, ẹ- [Elong]
A.15e *NENŲ*, n-
A.15f *KAA* [Bakaka]
Spoken also by the Mwahet [Manehas] and the Babɔŋ.
A.15g *MBƆ*
Spoken also by the Baneka, Bareko, and the Balɔndɔ.

LINGUISTIC FEATURES

This group strictly speaking lies outside the scope of this work, since it is covered by the report of the NBBS. Nevertheless for the sake of completeness an outline is given based mainly on the work by A. Bruens on A.11a Lundu. This language may be considered as typical of 11–14. The curious cluster of dialects numbered A.15 is in many respects in a category by itself owing to their peculiar phonology, but in other ways they can be considered as suitable for inclusion in this group. Where appropriate, some reference to them is made, based mainly on the material of H. Dorsch on 15*b*. Those interested in further details about this group are referred to the NBBS.

A. Sound Patterns

Closed syllables and final syllabic nasals appear to be rare in 11–14, although they do occur here and there, e.g. 14: **fįkǫl fįǹ** 'this knife'. In 15 however many syllables are closed, and syllabic nasals are common.

There is probably a simple series of seven radical vowels in 11–14, but in 15 centralized vowels occur.

In 11*a* there are certain rules governing vowel sequences between prefix and radical. There is only one mid front vowel and one mid back vowel in prefixes. These occur as ɛ or ɔ respectively when the vowel of the radical is ɛ or ɔ, but in other cases as ẹ or ọ, e.g. **ẹyọ** 'yam', **ɛyɔ** 'broom', where the first vowel is the same prefix in each case.

There are not many unusual consonants in these languages. It is clear that in 11*a* both **kw** and **kp** occur, but since in the available material the former occurs only in final syllables and the latter never, they may not in fact be distinct, e.g. **-kwa** 'receive', **-kpala** 'paddle'.

Tone appears to play an important part in all these languages, both as a lexical and as a grammatical feature. In the material given for 11*a*, however, tones are not marked since they are omitted in Bruen's work. In 13 and 14 tone-slip regularly occurs in verbals.

B. Class System

The following outline refers to 11*a*.

Independent Prefixes

Cl. 1/2	mo-/ba-	e.g. motįna/batįna	'old man/old men'
Cl. 3/4	mo-/me-	e.g. mǫlẹka/mẹlẹka	'youth/youths'
Cl. 5/6	dį-/ma-	e.g. dįlama/malama	'cheek/cheeks'
Cl. 7/8	e-/be-	e.g. ẹtụlį/bẹtụlį	'shoulder/shoulders'
Cl. 9/10	n-/n-	e.g. ndabǫ/ndabǫ	'house/houses'
Cl. 14/6	bo-/ma-	e.g. bǫlẹ/malẹ	'tree/trees'
Cl. 17	o-	e.g. ǫana	'mouth cavity'
Cl. 19/13	į-/lo-	e.g. įnɛ/lɔnɛ	'finger/fingers'

In vowel junction:

Cl. 1/2	ŋw-/b-	e.g. ŋwana/bana	'child/children'
Cl. 5/6	d-/m-	e.g. dǫ/mǫ	'voices/voices'
Cl. 14/6	w-/m-	e.g. walǫ/malǫ	'canoe/canoes'

With special stems:

In the case of certain words the vowel of the prefix is ʉ or ɨ; this unusual quality of vowel may be characteristic of the stem.

Cl. 3/4	mʉ-/mɨ-	e.g. mʉlɨ/mɨlɨ	'root/roots'
Cl. 14/4	bʉ-/mɨ-	e.g. bʉnya/mɨnya	'day/days'

A.10 LUNDU-MBO GROUP

Most of the other languages in this group have -ṵ- as the vowel of the prefix in Cl. 1 and Cl. 3, but in 15 there is usually a simple nasal consonant, e.g. 15*a* nlḛ́m 'heart'. Some of the other languages in this group have a larger proportion than usual of common words in Cl. 19/13.

In some of the dialects of 15 there are fewer classes than in the above list, in 15*b* for example, Cl. 8, 13, and 19 are missing.

Dependent Prefixes

Dependent prefixes in 11*a* are similar to the independent in shape, except in Cl. 9 and Cl. 10, e.g. manɛnɛ 'big ones (Cl. 6)', ɛnɛnɛ 'big one (Cl. 7 or Cl. 9)', inɛnɛ 'big one (Cl. 10 or Cl. 19)'.

An extra dependent prefix is linked with -a-, e.g. 14: djkyɛ́ dyákṵ́ba 'egg of the chicken'.

D. NUMERALS

In 11*a* the numerals '1'–'9' all consist of dependent nominals, but '6'–'9' are of the type '5' plus '1', &c. There is a special word ɔkɔrɔ '15', while a word do/mo 'score/scores' is used in the formation of all numerals from 20 to 199. For 200 upwards there is a special word jkɔlj '200', e.g. lɔkɔlj lọba na mọ mata '500'.

The other languages of the group mainly have a simple decimal system of counting, with independent nominals for '6'–'9'.

E. NOMINAL SENTENCES

In many cases nominal sentences are rare, although occasionally, as in the following example from A.13, there are sentences composed entirely of nominals.

    1. bwẹl bǫ́ń bọkɔlɔ 'this tree is big'
    2. mẹl máń makɔlɔ 'these trees are big'

F. VERBAL SYSTEM

The verbal systems of these languages are rather varied, so the following outline from 11*a* will serve as a general indication only.

Affirmative Conjugation

1. Remote Past	-mo-	-a	e.g. sjmọsaka	'we danced'
2. Near Past	-ma-	-a	e.g. sjmasaka	'we danced'
3. Near Future	—	-aka tj	e.g. sjsakaka tj	'we shall dance'
4. Remote Future	—	-aka	e.g. sjsakaka	'we shall dance'
5. Aspect of Completion	—	-j	e.g. sjsakj	'we have danced'
6. Aspect of Progress	-ne-	-a	e.g. sjnẹsaka	'we are dancing'
7. Aspect of Repetition	—	-aka	e.g. sjsakaka	'we dance'

Negative Conjugation

1. Past	-sjmo-	-a	e.g. sjsjmọsaka	'we did not dance'
2. Future	-sa-	-aka	e.g. sjsasakaka	'we shall not dance'
3. Aspect of Completion	-sa-	-j	e.g. sjsasakj	'we have not danced'
4. Aspect of Repetition	-sa-	-aka	e.g. sjsasakaka	'we do not dance'

An example of the importance of tone-patterns in 14 is provided by the following pair of tenses.

     ń'sọ́mbá 'I buy'
     ň'sọ́mbá 'I did not buy'

Personal Prefixes

The following list refers to 11a.

  Cl. 1. 1st: **na-** *or* **n-** 2nd: **o-** 3rd: **a-**
  Cl. 2. 1st: **sị-**   2nd: **nị-** 3rd: **ba-**

In 14 there are no special prefixes for the 1st and 2nd persons of Cl. 2, but in the dialects of 15 there are.

Object Substitutes

In 11a these are apparently separate words which follow the verbal.

  Cl. 1. 1st: **mba** 2nd: **ọẹ** 3rd: **mọ**
  Cl. 2. 1st: **sị**   2nd: **nyẹ** 3rd: **bọ**

Similar words for other classes are formed of a dependent prefix with -ọ, e.g. Cl. 19 **ịọ**.

Relative Constructions

These are introduced in many cases by a head-word consisting of a dependent prefix with -a, e.g. 14: **yê ndábọ yá balọ́ŋgị́** 'this is the house they built'.

G. Nomino-Verbals

In many of these languages nomino-verbals are in Cl. 5, e.g. 11a: **dịlọŋga** 'to build'.

H. Extensions

There do not appear to be many regular elements serving as extensions to radicals in these languages. The two following from 11a cannot be regarded as fully typical.

  Causative: **-ɛs-** e.g. **-bọl-/-bọlɛs-** 'work/employ'
  Passive: **-ab-** e.g. **-ọb-/-ọbab-** 'beat/be beaten'

K. Additional Observations

Vocabulary Content

These languages have a fairly large proportion of their vocabularies which is peculiar. In 11a there are, however, some items which are common to other Bantu languages outside the area, e.g. **-kọlw-** (← *-gùduk-) 'fly', **-ọb-** (← *-kúb-) 'hit'.

Sound Correspondences

Apart from the cluster 15, the correspondences of these languages are not very complicated. The following examples from 11a are typical of what occurs

  *t → l e.g. *-tín- → -lęn- 'cut'
  *d → zero e.g. *-dúmè → -mọmę 'husband'
  *k → zero e.g. *-kún- → -ọn- 'sow'
  *g → k e.g. *-gị → mọkị 'village'

A.10 LUNDU-MBO GROUP

Internal Relationships

The direction of reduction in the languages of this group is approximately as in the order of their numbering.

General Affinities

This group is clearly closely related to A.20, but it is possible that the cluster A.15 has some affinities with the nearby non-Bantu languages.

SOURCES

MS. notes on A.13 and A.14.
A.11: *Grammar of Lundu*, by A. Bruens, cyclostyled.
A.15b: 'Grammatik der Nkosi-Sprache', with 'Vocabularium der Nkosi-Sprache', by E. Dorsch, in *Z.f.K.S.*, 1911.

A.20 DUALA GROUP

A.21 BOMBOKO [Mboko]
Spoken in British Cameroons on the western slopes of Mount Cameroon by a small tribe.

A.22 BAAKPE [Bakwiri]
Spoken in British Cameroons on the southern slopes of Mount Cameroon by a small tribe.

A.23 SU [Isubu, Bimbia]
Spoken by a few people in the extreme south of British Cameroons.

A.24 DUALA
Spoken in Cameroun by some 22,000 people around the Douala estuary, and also used as a commercial language over a wider area.

A.25 OLI [Wuri, Ewodi]
Spoken in Cameroun by about 5,000 people along the lower reaches of the R. Wuri. The people called Bodiman also speak this language.

A.26 PODGO and MUDGO
These two dialects are spoken in Cameroun by some 10,000 people on both sides of the R. Mungo, near its mouth.

A.27 MULIMBA [Malimba]
Spoken by about 3,000 people in scattered settlements along the coast of Cameroun on both sides of the mouth of the R. Sanaga.

LINGUISTIC FEATURES

The type language is A.24 Dṵala.

A. Sound Patterns

Closed syllables apparently do not occur in these languages although in 24–27 a final syllabic nasal is fairly common, as in 24, e.g. dóm̀ '10'.

Throughout the group there is a simple series of seven radical vowels with no distinction of quantity.

The voiced stops are all imploded, a fact not indicated in the spelling of the examples. In 25 there is a voiced velar fricative, as e.g. mṵsɨya 'rope'.

In addition to two main levels of tone, rising and falling tones are regular features, particularly on final syllables, as in 24, e.g. adɨ 'he has found', atṵ 'he is poor'. Tone-slip occurs at the junction of certain elements as in 24, e.g. dɨmá'lóŋga 'we have already built'.

B. CLASS SYSTEM
Independent Prefixes
   The following list refers to 24.

    Cl. 1/2   mu̱-/ba-   e.g. mu̱ko̱rĥ/bako̱rĥ   'slave/slaves'
    Cl. 3/4   mu̱-/mi̱-   e.g. mu̱lé̱ma/mi̱lé̱ma   'heart/hearts'
    Cl. 5/6   -/ma-   e.g. dále̱/madále̱   'stone/stones'
    Cl. 7/8   e̱-/be̱-   e.g. e̱di̱má/be̱di̱má   'wall/walls'
    Cl. 9/10   n-/n-   e.g. ndábo̱/ndábo̱   'house/houses'
    Cl. 19/13   i̱-/lo̱-   e.g. i̱nɔń/lo̱nɔń   'bird/birds'
    Cl. 14/4   bo̱-/mi̱-   e.g. bo̱ló̱ŋgi̱/mi̱ló̱ŋgi̱   'building/buildings'

In vowel junction:
    Cl. 5/6   d-/m-   e.g. di̱na/mi̱na   'name/names'
               dʒ-/m-   e.g. dʒɔŋgɔ́/mɔŋgɔ́   'spear/spears'

The presence of -u̱- in the prefixes of Cl. 1 and Cl. 3 is confined to 24–27. The others have -o̱-.

Dependent Prefixes
There are several series of these, but for the most part their shape does not differ much from that of the independent prefixes. The following two are the more striking divergences that occur in 24 with a stem such as -pépɛ 'other', Cl. 1: nu̱-, Cl. 9: ni̱-.

An extra dependent prefix is linked with -a-, e.g. 24: dʒɔŋgɔ́ lamu̱bwé̱di̱ 'spear of the hunter'.

D. NUMERALS
There is a decimal system of counting, '1'–'5' being DN's and '6'–'9' IN's.

E. NOMINAL SENTENCES
These do not normally occur, as in the following examples from 26 there is usually a copula, in this case -e̱.

    1. mu̱ǹ mu̱hi̱ŋga mwé̱ bwabá   'this rope is long'
    2. mi̱ǹ mi̱hi̱ŋga mé̱ mi̱abá   'these ropes are long'

F. VERBAL SYSTEM
Conjugation
The following are the principal affirmative tenses in 24, the other languages having certain differences in their tense signs, but the same general type of conjugation.

    1. Past   —   -á e.g. di̱pu̱lá   'we dug'
    2. Future   -ni̱- -a e.g. di̱ni̱pu̱la   'we shall dig'
    3. Aspect of Completion   —   -i̱ e.g. di̱pu̱li̱   'we have dug'
    4. Aspect of Progress   -ma- -a e.g. di̱mapu̱la   'we are digging'

Negation
There is usually an identical series of negative verbals distinguished by the presence of a negative element, as -si̱- in 24, e.g. Tense 3. di̱si̱pu̱li̱ 'we have not dug'.

Personal Prefixes

There are only minor differences in the personal prefixes, so the following list from 24 is typical.

  Cl. 1 1st: **na-** 2nd: **ǫ-** 3rd: **a-**
  Cl. 2. 1st: **dị-** 2nd: **lǫ-** 3rd: **ba-**

The prefixes for other classes all have a high-tone except that in Cl. 9, **ę-**.

Relative Constructions

These have the same general characteristics throughout the group as in the following examples from 24.

(a) With an antecedent object. The verbal prefix has a high-tone, and there is a suffixed element -ˈnɔ́, e.g. **babǫlędị dịkakị-ˈnɔ́** 'workers we have hired'.

(b) With an antecedent subject. There are certain differences from the tones of simple verbals, and where simple tenses have a suffix -**a**, there is a suffix -**ɛ**. The dependent prefix used in these cases is nominal not verbal, e.g. **kę́ma nịˈmálandɛ̌** 'the monkey who climbs'.

G. Nomino-Verbals

These are usually in Cl. 5, e.g. 24: **dịpųla** 'to dig'.

H. Extensions

There are a number of regular extensions in these languages, although in certain cases it is not possible to quote the extension separately, the tense suffix having to be included. Here are some of the commonest types in 24.

  Applied: **-ę-** e.g. **-lǫ́ŋg/-lǫ́ŋgę-** 'build/build for'
  Causative: **-ɛ** e.g. **-lǫ́nd-/-lǫ́ndɛ** 'become full/fill'
  Instrumental: **-anɛ** e.g. **-tịl-/-tịlanɛ** 'write/write with'

K. Additional Observations

Vocabulary Content

There is not much common to the vocabularies of this group that does not also occur in other adjacent groups. These vocabularies contain very little that does not have the appearance of being of Bantu origin, nevertheless there is a relatively small proportion of them that can be related to items in Bantu languages elsewhere.

Sound Correspondences

In 24 the following correspondences occur and apart from that for *g are typical of the whole group.

  *p → w e.g. *-pácà → dịwásà 'twin'
  *t → l e.g. *-túk- → -lǫ́- 'abuse'
  *d → zero e.g. *-dànd- → -and- 'buy'
  *k → zero e.g. *-kúmị → dǫ́ṁ '10'
  *g → zero e.g. *-gàb- → -ab- 'divide'

In 22 there is the following correspondence which is more characteristic of Group A.40.

  A.22: *t → zero e.g. *-tábì → mǫawę 'branch'

A rather unusual correspondence that occurs in 25 is shown in the following example.

A.25: *-ŋg$_2$- → ɣ   e.g. *-gòŋgò → mɔyɔ   'back'

Internal Relationships

From some points of view this group can be regarded as falling into two subdivisions consisting of 21–23 and 24–27. Apart from this there is not much that can be said about the relative complexity of these languages.

General Affinities

There is a close relationship between this group and A.10 on the one side, and A.30 on the other. The apparent affinities between these languages and some in the north of Zone C is probably due to the very different nature of the intervening groups.

SOURCES

MS. notes on A.24–27.
A.22: 'Die Sprache der Bakwiri', by E. Schuler, in *M.S.O.S.* 1908.
A.23: 'Das Verbum in der Isubu-Sprache', by C. Meinhof, in *Z.A.S.* 1889.
A.24: *Wörterbuch der Duala-Sprache*, by E. Dinkelacker, 1914.
    Grammatik des Duala, by J. Ittman, 1939.

A.30 BUBE-BENGA GROUP

A.31 BỤBẸ [Ediya]
The dialects of this language are spoken in the island of Fernando Po.

A.32 BATANGA
A.32a BANƆƆ [Noko, Noho]
Spoken by some 2,000 people along the coast of Cameroun, near Kribi.
A.32b BAPỌKỌ [Naka, Puku]
Spoken by a very small group along the coast of Cameroun, near Grand Batanga.

A.33 YASA and KOMBE
Spoken along the coast of Cameroun and Rio Muni in scattered settlements by a small number of people.

A.34 BẸDGA
Spoken by small groups of people along the southern coast of Rio Muni, in the island of Corisco, and at Cap Esterias in Gabon.

LINGUISTIC FEATURES

There is so little reliable information about A.31 that is not possible to include anything about the linguistic features of these dialects. Also for A.33, beyond reports of similarity to A.32 and A.34 nothing certain is known. The type language for these notes is A.34 Bẹŋga.

A. Sound Patterns

Closed syllables apparently do not occur in these languages, and final syllabic nasals are uncommon.

There is a simple series of seven radical vowels with no distinction of quantity.

The consonants do not present any complications, although the voiced stops **b, d, j**, are all imploded, a fact not indicated in the spelling of the examples. The fricative sounds in 34 include β, ɣ, and **h**, the first of these being distinct from an implosive 'b', e.g. -βjny- 'wring', -bjn- 'refuse'. In 32 there is a simple labio-dental fricative, e.g. 32b jvọ 'river'.

There are two main levels of tone, rising and falling tones being uncommon. Tone-slip occurs regularly, examples from 34 being found in the negative conjugation.

B. Class System

There is not much variation in the classes of these languages, the following lists from 34 being typical.

Independent Prefixes

Cl. 1/2	mọ-/ba-	e.g. mọtọ/batọ	'person/persons'
Cl. 3/2	ụ-/ba-	e.g. ụtọdụ́/batọdụ́	'adult/adults'

Cl. 3/4	ụ-/mẹ-	e.g. ụkɔdị/mẹkɔdị	'rope/ropes'
Cl. 5/6	ị-/ma-	e.g. ịbɔ́ŋgɔ́/mabɔ́ŋgɔ́	'knee/knees'
Cl. 7/8	ẹ-/bẹ-	e.g. ẹhịkị́/bẹhịkị́	'forest/forests'
Cl. 9/10	n-/n-	e.g. mbanja/mbanja	'rib/ribs'
Cl. 14	bọ-	e.g. bọjọ́wá	'lie'
Cl. 19/13	ị-/lọ-	e.g. ịnɔnị́/lɔnɔnị́	'bird/birds'

In vowel junction:

Cl. 5/6	(i) ị-/m-	e.g. ịụmbá/mụmbá	'load/loads'
	(ii) d-/m-	e.g. dịhɔ/mịhɔ	'eye/eyes'
Cl. 14/4	(i) bụ-/mị-	e.g. bụálọ/mịálọ	'canoe/canoes'
	(ii) b-/mị-	e.g. bohọ́/mịohọ́	'face/faces'
Cl. 19/13	(i) βị-/l-	e.g. βịáha/láha	'orange/oranges'
	(ii) β-/l-	e.g. βeya/leya	'fire/fires'

With monosyllabic stems:

| Cl. 5/6 | dị-/ma- | e.g. dịtɔ́/matɔ́ | 'ear/ears' |
| Cl. 19 | βị- | e.g. βịyɔ́ | 'sleep' |

A peculiar feature in 32a is that the Cl. 13 prefix is vọ- (1- in vowel junction), e.g. ịyọ́/vọyọ́ 'river/rivers'.

Dependent Prefixes and Suffixes

There are several series of dependent nominal elements in these languages. The dependent prefixes in 34 are mostly similar in shape to the independent prefixes, except in the case of Cl. 9 ẹ-, Cl. 10 ị-, Cl. 19 βị-.

An extra dependent prefix is attached with -a-, e.g. 32a: jɔ́mbɛ dándábọ 'roof of the house'.

D. NUMERALS

There is a simple decimal system of counting, '1'–'5' being DN's and '6'–'9' IN's. The word for '10' jọ́mụ, is, however, not used in multiples, instead there is a word in Cl. 6 based on a different stem as in 34, e.g. mabọ́ mábalẹ '20'.

E. NOMINAL SENTENCES

These do not appear to occur in this group. In the following examples from 32b it will be seen that the copula is not followed by a dependent nominal in the same class as the rest of the sentence, but by an independent nominal in Cl. 14. This is typical of these languages.

1. yẹlẹ́ tɛyẹ́ ẹ̀ndị bọnɛ́nɛ   'this tree is big'
2. bẹlẹ́ tɛbé bẹ́ǹdị bọnɛ́nɛ   'these trees are big'

F. VERBAL SYSTEM

There is much similarity between the verbal systems of these languages, so the following outline based on 34 can be taken as typical.

1. Remote Past   —   -ákịǹdị   e.g. họ́hámbákịǹdị 'we bought'
2. Near Past   -ma-   -àǹdị   e.g. họ́mahámbàǹdị 'we bought'

3. Near Future	-ka-	-ándj́	e.g. hǫ́kahámbándj́	'we shall buy'
4. Remote Future	-ka-	-andj́	e.g. hǫ́kahámbandj́	'we shall buy'
5. Aspect of Completion	—	-j́ndj́	e.g. hǫ́hámbj́ndj́	'we have bought'
6. Aspect of Progress	—	-ákandj́	e.g. hǫ́hámbákandj́	'we are buying'

In those tenses where -a- is shown in the tense suffix, certain radicals regularly have -ɛ- instead, e.g. -yál- 'begin', hómayálḗndj́ 'we began'.

Negative Conjugation

1. Remote Past	-ų́- -áká	e.g. hų́hámbáká	'we did not buy'
2. Recent Past	-ų́- -á	e.g. hų́hámbá	'we did not buy'
3. Future	-a- -ẹ	e.g. hwâhámbẹ	'we shall not buy'
4. Aspect of Progress	-a- -aka	e.g. hwâhámbaka	'we are not buying'

Personal Prefixes

The following list refers to 34.

    Cl. 1. 1st: **na-**   2nd: **ǫ-**   3rd: **a-**
    Cl. 2. 1st: **hǫ-**   2nd: **ǫ- -nj́**   3rd: **ba-**

In 32a the prefix for the 1st person of Cl. 2 is **j́-**. In this language there is also a special agreement for words with an extra prefix, e.g. ǫ́ndábǫ ǫ́dj namẁέŋgj́ 'at the house is a stranger'.

Object Substitutes

The following typical notes refer to 34.

    Cl. 1. 1st: **-mba**   2nd: **-bɛ**   3rd: **-mɔ**
    Cl. 2. 1st: **-hwẹ**   2nd: **j́nyɛnj́**   3rd: **-bɔ**

For other classes the O.S. is formed of a concord element plus **-ɔ**, e.g. **-bjɔ** (Cl. 8). Each of these substitutes except that for the second person of Cl. 2 is affixed to the verbal which then does not have the element **-ndj́**, e.g. hǫ́hámbákj́ndj́ 'we bought', hóhámbákj́-bjɔ 'we bought them'.

Relative Constructions

These are similar in both languages, but the following refers to 34.

(a) With an antecedent subject. An element **-dj́** occurs in place of **-ndj́** shown in the above list, e.g. **bándj́ báhámbákj́dj́ bẹbų́ŋgụ** 'they are those who bought the mats'.

(b) With an antecedent object. There is a special construction in which the verbal agrees with the antecedent, while the nominal referring to the logical subject is brought into relation with the antecedent by means of an extra dependent prefix with **-a-**, e.g. **bę́ndj́ bẹbų́ŋgụ bj́ábána bę́mahámbá** 'they are the mats the children bought'.

G. NOMINO-VERBALS

These are in Cl. 5, e.g. 32: **j́vέvɛ** 'to fly'.

H. Extensions

The rules governing the relationship between extended radicals and simple radicals are rather complicated, but the following examples from 34 will illustrate some of these.

Applied: -į-, e.g. -hámb-/-hámbį- 'buy/buy for'
With tense affixes containing -ak- the extension follows -ak-, while -ę- occurs instead of -į-, e.g. Negative Tense 1: hųhámbákįá-bɔ 'we did not buy for them', Aff. Tense 5: hǫhámbįę́-bɔ 'we have bought for them'.

In the following two cases -ɛ- always occurs where -a- is shown in the tense suffixes.

        Causative: -įd-   e.g. -hámb/--hámbįd- 'buy/sell'
        Passive: -w-   e.g. -lǫ́ŋg-/-lǫ́ŋgw-   'build/be built'

This latter extension also follows -ak-, and in those tenses where there is an element -į-, -ǫdwę- occurs for the extension plus -į-, e.g. Aff. Tense 5: ęlǫ́ŋgǫ́dwę́ṅdį 'it (Cl. 9) has been built'.

K. Additional Observations

Vocabulary Content

There are many peculiar items in these languages, although there is an average proportion that can be related to those elsewhere in the Bantu area.

Sound Correspondences

The following correspondences are the most noteworthy in 34.

        *p → β   e.g. *-pí-   → -β́ę- 'become ripe'
        *t → l   e.g. *-túŋg- → -lǫ́ŋg- 'build'
        *d → zero e.g. *-dámb- → -ámb- 'cook'

General Affinities

These languages show a close relationship with A.20 and a lesser one to B.10. There is little affinity between this group and the nearby A.70 and A.80 languages.

SOURCES

MS. notes on A.32 and A.34.
A.31: 'Beiträge zur Kentniss der Bube-Sprache', by O. Baumann, in *Z.A.S.* 1887.
A.34: *Grammar of the Benga-Bantu Language*, by R. H. Nassau, 1892.

A.40 BASA GROUP

A.41 LƆMBĮ [Rombi]
Spoken by a small tribe in British Cameroons, not far from the Nigerian border.

A.42 BADKỌN [Abo]
Spoken by some 10,000 people in two groups, one being just on the border between British Cameroons and Cameroun and the other astride the R. Abo, to the south-east of Mbanga.

A.43 BASA

A.43a MBƐNƐ [Basa, Koko, Mvele]
Spoken over a large area to the north-east and east of Douala, by some 150,000 people.

A.43b BAKƆGƆ [Koko]
Spoken by about 20,000 people just in from the coast to the north and south of Douala.

A.44 BANƐN [Banend]
Spoken by about 24,000 people, who are divided into a large number of small sub-tribes, to the south-west of Ndikinineki.

A.45 NYƆ̃'Ɔ̃ [Nyokon]
Spoken by about 3,000 people on the fringe of the Bantu-speaking area, to the north-west of Ndikinineki.

A.46 MANDĮ [Lemande]
Spoken by about 4,000 people to the north-west of Bafia. The people known as Yambeta and Bonek also speak this language.

LINGUISTIC FEATURES

The type language is A.43a Mbɛnɛ.

A. Sound Patterns

Closed syllables are very common in all positions, many words consisting of one such syllable, as in 43a, e.g. **mįs** 'eyes', **ǵwĕt** 'war'. In 46 there are unusual closed syllables of the following type, **ọntʃ** 'woman', **atw** 'head', **ǿly** 'moon'. Non-final closed syllables also occur, apparently giving rise to unusual consonant clusters in medial position, as in 43a, e.g. **-gl-** as in **-soɡla** 'be peeled', **-nb-** as in **-kanba** 'be split'. Final syllabic nasals are also extremely common, as in 43a, e.g. **wɔrṁ** 'garden', **lįkɔŋ** 'spear'.

There is a series of seven radical vowels in each language, but in 44 and 46 centralization is common. Long and short vowels also occur in 43, but it is not certain that there are two distinct quantities in vowels.

There are complicated rules of vowel sequences in these languages. In 46 for example there is a pair of prefixes which appear as a-/bɛ- when the radical vowel is a, ẹ, or ọ, but as ɛ-/bị- when it is ɛ, as ɔ-/bɛ- when it is ɔ, and as ẹ-/bị- when it is ị or ụ.

A final stop is frequently not fully released, while in this position there is no distinction between voiced and voiceless stops. The voiced bilabial stop written 'b' in all the following examples from 43a is imploded when it occurs initially or intervocalically.

Tone is an important feature, often distinguishing items, as in 43a, e.g. -lɛb 'mourn', -lɛ́b 'throw away'. Tone-slip frequently occurs, as may be seen by referring to the verbal conjugation.

B. CLASS SYSTEM

Independent Prefixes

The following list refers to 43a.

Cl. 1/2	n-/ba-	e.g. nlǫ́m̀/balǫ́m̀	'man/men'
Cl. 1a/2a	mụ-/bọ-	e.g. mụdǎ/bọdǎ	'wife/wives'
Cl. 3/4	n-/mịn-	e.g. ŋkụ́lɛŋ/mịŋkụ́lɛŋ	'axe/axes'
Cl. 5/6	lị-/ma-	e.g. lịkɔŋ́/makɔŋ́	'spear/spears'
Cl. 7/8	-/bị-	e.g. sɛl/bịsɛl	'basket/baskets'
Cl. 9/10	n-/n-	e.g. ŋgań/ŋgań	'crocodile/crocodiles'
Cl. 11/6	-/ma-	e.g. lẹ́p/malẹ́p	'well/wells'
Cl. 19/13	hị-/dị-	e.g. hịnụnị́/dịnụnị́	'bird/birds'

In vowel junction:

Cl. 1/2	ŋw-/b-	e.g. ŋwǎ/bǎ	'woman/women'
Cl. 5/6	j-/m-	e.g. jǒl/mǒl	'nose/noses'
Cl. 11/4	ŋw-/ŋw-	e.g. ŋwěl/ŋwěl	'tail/tails'
	w-/ŋw-	e.g. wɔm̀/ŋwɔm̀	'garden/gardens'
Cl. 19/13	hy-/ty-	e.g. hyɔŋ/tyɔŋ	'hair/hairs'

The most notable difference in the prefixes of the other languages is in 44 and 46 where the Cl. 5 prefix is nị- (or nɛ-) and nyị- (or nyɛ-) respectively. In each of these languages there is a high proportion of common words in Cl. 19/13.

Dependent Prefixes

There is considerable variety in the series of dependent prefixes occurring in 43a with different kinds of words. The following examples will serve as an illustration: Cl. 1/2 nụ́nụ́/báná 'this/these', wɛ́m̀/bɛ́m̀ 'my', nnáǹ/banáǹ 'your (pl.)'. Cl. 9 and Cl. 10 in certain cases are distinct only in tone, e.g. ịnị́/ịnị́ 'this/these'. Cl. 3 and Cl. 14 are similar in some cases, but not in all, e.g. ŋkɛ́nị́ 'big one (Cl. 3, 14)', wɛ́m̀ 'my (Cl. 3 and Cl. 14)', but nụ́nụ́ 'this (Cl. 3)', ụ́nụ́ 'this (Cl. 14)'.

An extra dependent prefix is attached with no linking vowel, as in 43a, e.g. hịbě hịmụ́dǎ 'the pot of the wife'.

D. NUMERALS

There is a simple decimal system of counting, '1'–'7' being dependent nominals, but '8' and '9' independent.

E. NOMINAL SENTENCES

In these languages, nominal sentences are rare, in most cases a copula is used, such as -áŋ in the following examples from 46.
1. bɔty ɨpw áŋ pwaŋ   'this tree is big'
2. maty əm máŋ maŋ   'these trees are big'

F. VERBAL SYSTEM

The verbal systems of these languages vary considerably. The following outline refers to 43a and gives a general idea only of what occurs in the group.

Conjugation

1. Remote Past   -ˈ   e.g. djpɔ́t/báˈpɔ́t   'we/they spoke'
2. Near Past   -bjˈ-   e.g. djbjˈpɔ́t   'we spoke'
3. Future   -áˈ-   e.g. daáˈpɔ́t/baáˈpɔ́t   'we/they shall speak'
4. Aspect of Completion   -m-   e.g. djmpɔ́t/bámpɔ́t   'we/they have spoken'
5. Aspect of Progress   -ḿˈ-   e.g. djḿˈpɔ́t/bámˈpɔ́t   'we/they are speaking'
6. Past Aspect of Repetition -ˈ -ák   e.g. djpɔ́rɔ́k   'we used to speak'

The affix in Tenses 4 and 5 occurs as -ŋ- or -ŋw- with those radicals that commence with a vowel, e.g. djŋɔ́m 'we have sent'.

The affix in Tense 6, shown as -ak, occurs in a number of different shapes dependent upon the shape of the radical, e.g. -lɔ/-lɔ̌k 'come', -kẹs/-kẹhę́k 'put', -pų́ẉɛ/-pų́ų́gę́ 'fly', -bę́dẹs/-bę́dhák 'lift', -lana/-langá 'bring'. Similar affixes occur in all the other languages of the group.

In 46 there is a most unusual feature in the word division of verbals, e.g.

    bánátɨmə́k   'they are digging'
    tɔfɛ   'holes'
    bána tɔfya tɨmə́k   'they are digging holes'

In cases like this, not only does the nominal object precede the verbal base, but at the junction there are additional sounds in current speech which are not heard in deliberate speech.

Negation

There are no special negative tenses in 43a, but a negative element -ˈbę́ę́ occurs attached to the verbal in each tense, e.g. djbjˈpɔ́t-ˈbę́ę́ 'we did not speak', djbjˈɔ́m-bę́ę́ ǵwɔ́ḿ 'we did not send the things'.

In 44 and 46 there are special negative tenses.

A.40 BASA GROUP

Personal Prefixes

The following list refers to 43a.

Cl. 1. 1st: **mɛ-** 2nd: **ṷ-** 3rd: **a-**
Cl. 2. 1st: **dį-** 2nd: **nį-** 3rd: **ba-**

The prefixes for the other classes in this language all have a high-tone except that for Cl. 9, e.g. **į-**.

Copula

The following forms of the copula in 43a are interesting, in that they are formed with elements similar to those occurring in languages in other parts of Bantu-speaking Africa.

1. Remote Past   -bá¹   e.g. abá¹ háná   'he was here'
2. Near Past   -bę́ę   e.g. abę́ę háná   'he was here yesterday'
3. Immediate Past -bák   e.g. abák háná   'he was here today'
4. Future   -á¹bá¹ e.g. aá¹bá¹ háná 'he will be here'
5. Zero Time   -yę   e.g. ayę háná   'he is here'

G. NOMINO-VERBALS

In 42 and 43 there are nomino-verbals in Cl. 7, e.g. 42: **įsálak** 'to work'. In 44 and 46 nomino-verbals have a prefix **ǫ-** (or **ɔ-**) e.g. 44: **ɔnyá** 'to drink'.

H. EXTENSIONS

There are a number of regular extensions in these languages although the rules for the relationship of extended radicals to simple radicals are often very complicated. The following are some of the more important extensions in 43a.

1. Applied: -(v)l, -lɛ, -ɛ e.g. -nɔl/-nɔlɔl 'laugh/laugh at', -ɔ́m/-ɔ́mlɛ 'send/send to', -tɔŋɔl/-tɔŋlɛ 'explain/explain to'.

2. Causative: -(v)s with closing of the radical vowel, e.g. -bɔl/-bǫlǫs 'become rotten/rot', -hend/-hįndįs 'become black/blacken'.

3. Reversive: -(v)l with closing of the radical vowel, except -a-, e.g. -teŋ/-tįŋįl 'tie/untie', -kaŋ/-kaŋal 'bind/unbind'.

4. Neuter: -ba, -a, e.g. -bǫk/-bǫkba 'break/become broken', -sǫgǫl/-sǫgla 'peel/become peeled', -kan/-kanba 'split/become split'.

5. Passive: -a with closing of the radical vowel, e.g. -ɔ́m/-ǫ́ma 'send/be sent', -bep/-bįba 'hit/be hit', -kaŋ/-kęŋa 'bind/be bound'.

K. ADDITIONAL OBSERVATIONS

Vocabulary Content

Although superficially the vocabularies of these languages appear to contain many peculiar items, there is nevertheless a relatively high proportion corresponding to those in languages outside the area. In a number of cases, however, it seems likely that there are items of non-Bantu origin.

Sound Correspondences

The rules governing the correspondences of the sounds in some of these languages are complicated. The following four examples from 43a will illustrate the kind of consonant correspondences that occur.

*t → zero	e.g.	*-táŋg- →	-áŋ	'read'
*d → l	e.g.	*-dób- →	-lɔ́p	'fish'
*k → h	e.g.	*-kúd- →	-hɔ́l	'grow up'
*ġ → k	e.g.	*-ġàŋġ- →	-kaŋ	'tie up'

In 41–43 there is extensive occurrence of umlaut. The following examples will illustrate the kind of thing that happens in 43a, and will demonstrate that the seven radical vowels of this language do not correspond in a simple way to the seven starred vowels.

*-u̯- -a → -o-	e.g. *-ku̯bà → kóp	'chicken'
*-u- -a → -ɔ-	e.g. *-gùmbà → kɔm	'barren woman'
*-a- -i → -ɛ-	e.g. *-yátì → nyĕt	'buffalo'

Internal Relationships

Although the languages of this group are closely related to one another, it is difficult to describe their relationship in terms of complexity and reduction, apart from saying that 45 is the most reduced member.

General Affinities

This group is peculiar in many ways. It displays certain Bantu features that do not commonly occur in this area, at the same time as having what are apparently unusual characteristics. Although the shape of many of its words is reminiscent of what is found in A.70, it is doubtful whether there is a close affinity with that group. In effect the relationships of these languages to others in the area are very difficult to determine.

SOURCES

MS. notes on A.42–44, 46.
A.42: *Die Sprache der Bǫ oder Bankon*, by F. Spellenberg, 1922.
A.43a: *Die Sprache der Basa in Kamerun*, by G. Schurle, 1912.

A.50 BAFIA GROUP

A.51 *FA'*, lə- [Fak, Balom]

Spoken in Cameroun, on both sides of the R. Mbam, north of its confluence with the R. Noun, by nearly 4,000 people.

A.52 *KAALOD*, lə- or *MBƆD*, lə-

Spoken on the south bank of the R. Mbam just below its confluence with the R. Noun, by a handful of people.

A.53 *KPA*, rə- [Bafia]

Spoken round about and to the south-west of Bafia in Cameroun by about 12,000 people.

A.54 *DGAYABA*, lə- [Djanti]

Spoken by under 1,000 people on the eastern side of the Djanti hills, to the north-east of Bafia in Cameroun.

LINGUISTIC FEATURES

The type language is A.52 Kaaloŋ or Mbɔŋ.

A. Sound Patterns

One peculiar feature of the patterns in these languages is that many words have no vowel at all, e.g. 51: **-yŋ́** 'run', 52: **fnsm fñ** 'this knife', **dyk** 'egg'.

Closed syllables are very common in all positions within sentences, as in 52, e.g. **lip** 'plain', **mwẹt** 'sun'.

The vowel qualities are very complicated and centralized and nasalized vowels are extremely common, while varieties of vowel with constriction of the pharynx also occur. In all the examples quoted for 52 the vowel represented by 'ï' is a high central vowel. There are two quantities of vowel in final radical position in these languages, e.g. 52: **lidṹ** 'knee', **libṹṹ** 'sky', but the rules governing the incidence of long vowels in non-final position are not very clear.

Tone is an important feature of these languages, frequently serving to distinguish otherwise identical items, e.g. 52: **nʒḭ́** 'tail', **nʒḭ̀** 'pig'. Examples of the occurrence of tone-slip may be seen in the conjugation.

B. Class System

There is much similarity between the class systems of these languages, in particular the occurrence of many common words in Cl. 19/13. The following outline is from 52.

Independent Prefixes

Cl. 1/2	various	e.g. **man/bwɔn**	'child/children'
		gïp/bëyïp	'woman/women'
Cl. 3/4	n-/mə-	e.g. **ntɔ́/mətɔ́**	'head/heads'

Cl. 5/6	li-/mə-	e.g. likɔŋ/məkɔŋ	'spear/spears'
Cl. 7/8	gi-/bi-	e.g. gikɔ́ṁ/bikɔ́ṁ	'canoe/canoes'
Cl. 9/10	n-/n-	e.g. mbəŋ/mbəŋ	'wound/wounds'
Cl. 19/13	fi-/di-	e.g. fidɔ́p/didɔ́p	'fishhook/fishhooks'

In vowel junction:

Cl. 3/4	mu̧-/mj-	e.g. mu̧ɔm/mjɔm	'mouth/mouths'
Cl. 7/8	tʃ-/by-	e.g. tʃɛsɔ/byɛsɔ	'broom/brooms'
Cl. 19/13	fy-/ty-	e.g. fyɛ́n/tyɛ́n	'leaf/leaves'

Dependent Prefixes

There are several series of dependent prefixes, but for the most part, the shape of these prefixes is the same as that of the independent prefixes. The following are the most important exceptions to this in 52; Cl. 3. wu̧-, Cl. 9 and Cl. 10. yi-.

An extra dependent prefix is attached with no linking vowel, e.g. 52: **tyɛ́ń djbití** 'leaves of the trees'.

D. NUMERALS

The numerals of these languages are very similar, and the following details from 52 are typical of them all. '1'–'5' consist of dependent nominals, but there are invariable words for '6'–'9' of the following pattern, **tânjṅ** '9', where -njṅ is identical in shape with the stem of the numeral '4'. There is a special word **litjṅ** for '20' which is used in the formation of all higher numerals.

E. NOMINAL SENTENCES

These regularly occur in each language, with a peculiarity which is seen most clearly in 52. In this language a plural sentence has -g suffixed to the stable word, e.g.

1. **gití kṅ ktɔ́ɔ́**   'this tree is big'
2. **bití bṅ btɔ́ɔ́g**   'these trees are big'

F. VERBAL SYSTEM

The verbal systems do not vary much from language to language. The chief feature to be noted is that there are two different bases used for each tense according as the event is singular or plural. The sign of the plural base is a suffix **-ak**, as in the following examples from 52.

ăkabí diɣŋ   'he has sold a pot'
dăkabí gikɔ́ṁ   'we have sold a canoe'
ăkafák məyŋ   'he has sold pots'

The following outline of the tenses from 52 may be regarded as typical of the whole group.

Affirmative Conjugation

1. Remote Past	-má¹- -í	e.g. dimáleɛgí/dimáleɛgák	'we sewed'
2. Recent Past	-ń¹- -í	e.g. diṅleɛgí/diṅleɛgák	'we sewed'
3. Future	—¹	e.g. díleɛk/díleɛgak	'we shall sew'

A.50 BAFIA GROUP

4. Aspect of Completion	-ă- -í	e.g. dălɛɛgí/dăleɛgák		'we have sewed'
5. Aspect of Progress	—	e.g. díilɛɛk/díilɛɛgak		'we are sewing'

Negative Conjugation

1. Past	-â- -wǫ́	e.g. dâlɛɛgwǫ́/dâlɛɛgágwǫ́	'we did not sew'
2. Future	-ăbá¹-	e.g. dăbálɛɛk/dăbálɛɛgák	'we shall not sew'
3. Aspect of Progress	-ăbání-	e.g. dăbánílɛɛk/dăbánílɛɛgak	'we are not sewing'

Personal Prefixes

The following list refers to 52, but the differences in the other languages are slight.

Cl. 1.   1st: **n-**   2nd: **ṵ-**   3rd: **a-**
Cl. 2.   1st: **di-**   2nd: **bi-**   3rd: **bɛ-**

G. NOMINO-VERBALS

These are in Cl. 5, e.g. 52: **lidaa** 'to buy'.

H. EXTENSIONS

There are no clear extensions in any of these languages.

K. ADDITIONAL OBSERVATIONS

Vocabulary Content

From the available material it is clear that there is a large number of items common to these languages that cannot be related to those of other Bantu languages outside the group. There are sufficient items to justify including languages of this kind as Bantu, but it must be admitted that they almost constitute a border-line case.

Sound Correspondences

Even where corresponding words can be found, the rules governing the correspondences of the sounds are very obscure.

Internal Relationships

The direction of the reduction of features appears to be approximately in the order of the numbering of the languages, although it is not clear whether 51 or 53 is the more complex.

General Affinities

These languages have most affinity with Group A.70, and little with A.40 or A.60. Despite the superficial similarity in their sound patterns, it is doubtful whether they have a close relationship with A.80.

SOURCES

MS. notes for the whole group.
Die Bafia und die Kultur der Mittelkamerun Bantu, by G. Tessmann, 1934, contains a tribal map and a few linguistic notes on A.53.

A.60 SANAGA GROUP

THE languages of this group are spoken mainly round about the two rivers Mbam and Sanaga, near their confluence. Apparently they are spoken by the peoples referred by Tessmann as Bati-Mbam.

A.61 *ŊGƆRƆ*

Spoken in Cameroun by a small group of people to the north-east of Bafia.

A.62 *YAMBASA*

Spoken in Cameroun by about 25,000 people to the south of Bafia, on the west side of the rivers Mbam and Sanaga.

A.63 *MAŊGJSA*

Spoken in Cameroun in the curve of the R. Sanaga above its confluence with the R. Mbam, by about 14,000 people.

A.64 *BACƐŊGA* [Betsinga]

Spoken in Cameroun on the north side of the R. Sanaga, above its confluence with the R. Mbam, by about 10,000 people.

A.65 *BATI*

Spoken in Cameroun by a small group of people along the west bank of the R. Lihoua, near its confluence with the R. Sanaga.

LINGUISTIC FEATURES

The type language is A.62 Yambasa.

A. SOUND PATTERNS

Cases of closed syllables have been observed, e.g. 62: **sjɔt** '10'; 63: **ntʃélék** 'sand', but this kind of pattern is not very common.

There is a simple series of seven radical vowels with no distinction of vowel quantity in each language.

One notable feature common to the group is that certain sequences of vowels are impossible, the following typical example being from 62. The sequences -j- -a and -ʯ- -a do not occur, but where they would be expected, -ɛ occurs, e.g. **nyjmɛ́** 'back', **mɛgʯ́dɛ** 'oil'. As between a pre-radical syllable and the radical syllable, the sequences -a- -j-, -a- -ʯ-, do not occur, but where they would be expected -ɛ- occurs in pre-radical position, e.g. **ɛ̀ŋgjsɔ** 'eyes'. The consonant sounds are simple on the whole, the voiced stops being exploded.

Tone is an important feature serving to distinguish many items, as in 62, e.g. **-ǫ́y-** 'boil', **-ǫy-** 'say'. Tone-slip appears to occur in 63 and 64 at certain grammatical junctions.

A.60 SANAGA GROUP

B. CLASS SYSTEM
Independent Prefixes

In these languages there is a peculiar excess of independent prefixes. In the following list from 62 there are two prefixes which cannot be directly related to those of languages outside the group, which are given the symbols X and Y instead of figures.

Cl. 1/2	ṷ-/ba-	e.g. ṷhaŋa/bahaŋa	'youth/youths'
Cl. 3/4	ọ-/ẹ-	e.g. ọmbɔ́gɔ/ẹmbɔ́gɔ	'arm/arms'
Cl. 5/6	ẹ-/aṉ-	e.g. ẹbányɛ/ambányɛ	'breast/breasts'
Cl. 7/8	ģị-/bị-	e.g. ģịnamá/bịnamá	'leg/legs'
Cl. 9/10	ṉ-/ṉ-	e.g. ntʃų́bɛ/ntʃų́bɛ	'chicken/chickens'
Cl. 11/13	nṷ-/dṷ-	e.g. nṷɛlị́/dṷɛlị́	'rope/ropes'
Cl. 14/X	bọ-/ma-	e.g. bọbámá/mabámá	'plank/planks'
Cl. 15/X	ģṷ-/ma-	e.g. ģṷkánya/makánya	'pain/pains'
Cl. 16.	ha-	e.g. hɔɔ́ma	'place'
Cl. 19/Y	ị-/mṷ-	e.g. ịléŋų́/mṷléŋų́	'axe/axes'

In vowel junction:
  Cl. 5. nj- e.g. njɔlɔ́ 'neck'
  Cl. 6. In this case the prefix together with the stem occurs as aŋg-, the prefix vowel following the usual rules of vowel sequence, e.g. aŋgɔlɔ́ 'necks', njísɔ/ɛŋgísɔ 'eye/eyes'.

The classes in 63 are more unusual in that the singular/plural correlation is not fixed, but may be reversed in some cases, as for example in the following pairs where the peculiar prefix tɛ- occurs:

tɛpapá/apapá	'wing/wings'
apų́pų́/tɛpų́pų́	'garden/gardens'
tɛkɔŋgɔ́/tɛkɔŋgɔ́	'spear/spears'

Dependent Prefixes

There are several series of dependent prefixes, which do not present any particular difficulty. It is interesting to note that the word hɔɔ́ma 'place' in 62, can have either the agreement of Cl. 16 or one similar to Cl. 15, e.g. hááha hámẹ or gɔ́ɔ́gɔ gámẹ 'this (place) is mine'.

An extra dependent prefix is attached with -a-. This vowel obeys the rule of vowel sequence, as in 62, e.g. ịdɔ́ŋɔ hanyádẹ 'tail of the buffalo', ịdɔ́ŋɔ hɛmbų́nyị 'tail of the goat'.

D. NUMERALS

In 62 the numerals '1'–'9' consist of dependent nominals, but '6'–'9' are of the type '5' plus '1', while numerals above '20' are based on a system of score counting. In 64 on the other hand, '1'–'5' are dependent nominals, while '6' and '8' are independent, '7' being '6' plus '1', and '9', '8' plus '1'. There is also a special word bwẹŋgɔ́ '15'.

E. Nominal Sentences

These do not usually occur, some kind of copula, like -lį in these examples from 62, is normally used.

1. nμɛlį nɔ́ɔ́nɔ nų́lį nọntaálala
2. dμɛlį dɔ́ɔ́dɔ dų́lį dọntaálala

F. Verbal System

Conjugation

The verbal system varies from language to language, but the following list of tenses from 62 may be taken as typical.

1. Remote Past	-mba-	-a	e.g. djmbɛdįmɛ	'we dug'
2. Near Past	-a-	-á	e.g. djɛdįmɛ́	'we dug'
3. Future	-ná-	-a	e.g. djnɛ́dįmɛ	'we shall dig'
4. Aspect of Progress	—	-a	e.g. djdįmɛ	'we are digging'

Negation

There is an identical series of negative verbals in 62, distinguished by the presence of an element -dj- following the dependent prefix, e.g. djdjnɛ́dįmɛ 'we shall not dig'.

In 63 on the other hand negation is expressed by means of a special negative radical -tam.

Personal Prefixes

Here is the list for 62, there being a number of differences in the other languages.

    Cl. 1.   1st: **n-**   2nd: **μ-**   3rd: **a-**
    Cl. 2.   1st: **dj-**   2nd: **nμ-**   3rd: **ba-**

Object Substitutes

Apart from the first person of Cl. 1 there is a surprising difference in 62 in the shape of the object substitute and the personal prefix, e.g.:

    Cl. 1.   1st: **-n-**   2nd: **-ga-**   3rd: **-mμ-**
    Cl. 2.   1st: **-tʃμ-**   2nd: **-nyμ-**   3rd: **-bμ-**

G. Nomino-Verbals

The nomino-verbals in 62 are in Cl. 15, e.g. **gμbána** 'to marry'.

H. Extensions

The extensions in these languages are not very regular, but the following example from 62 illustrates two kinds that commonly occur.

    Causative: **-j-**   e.g. **-djaŋ-/-djɛnj-**   'become spoilt/spoil'
                   -anj-   e.g. **-jlɛb-/-jlɛbɛnj-**   'become black/blacken'

K. Additional Observations

Vocabulary Content

The vocabularies of these languages are interesting in that a large proportion of them is common to the group. In addition there are a number of items related to those elsewhere in the Bantu field which do not appear to occur in adjacent groups, as the following from 62, e.g.:

-hų́m- (← *-pų́m-)	'go out'
įsɛ́ (←*-yįcé)	'father'
ugǫ́nǫ́ (← *-kúdù)	'adult'
*-gɔ́gįd- (← *-kók-)	'pull'

Sound Correspondences

The following correspondences for consonants from 62 are typical of the whole group.

*t → d	e.g. -tímà → ọdę́má	'heart'
*d → n	e.g. -dámb- → -námb-	'cook'
*k → g̣	e.g. -kádį → ụgánį́	'woman'

Internal Relationships

The most complex member of the group is probably A.62, and the most reduced A.64, but there is not very much difference between the members of the group from this point of view.

General Affinities

In many respects this group is one on its own and does not display much relationship with the adjacent ones. Although it is difficult to demonstrate, nevertheless there is much about these languages which seems to suggest that they represent a mingling of two distinct sources, one of which appears to have affinities with Bantu languages right outside the area.

SOURCES

MS. notes on A.61–64.
A.65: A few notes are gives in 'Die Sprachverhältnisse in Kamerun', by C. Meinhof, in *Z.A.O.S.* 1895.

A.70 YAUNDE-FANG GROUP

This is the largest group of languages in the whole of the area dealt with in this work, there being probably 700,000 people who speak these languages.

A.71 ETON

Spoken in Cameroun by over 110,000 people in a thickly populated area to the north-west of Yaounde.

A.72 EWONDO and MVELE

A.72a EWONDO [Yaunde]

Spoken in Cameroun by about 95,000 people to the south-west of Yaounde in the direction of Lolodorf and of the coast. The most westerly group of people speaking this language are known as Evuzok.

A.72b MVELE

This dialect is spoken in Cameroun by a very large number of different peoples to the east of Yaounde, in the direction of Akonolinga and Nanga-Eboko. Altogether there are nearly 140,000 speakers of this language divided between many different sub-tribes, including Omvaŋ.

A.72c BAKJA [Badjia]

Spoken in Cameroun to the south-east of Nanga-Eboko by about 14,000 people, some of whom are known as Yekaba.

A.72d YADGAFƆK

A very scattered group of peoples in Cameroun speak this dialect, which also includes the one known as Bafök, mainly in enclaves among the speakers of non-Bantu languages, there being about 5,000 in all.

A.73 BĔBĔLĔ and GBĬGBĬL

A.73a BĔBĔLĔ [Bamvele]

Spoken in Cameroun by about 18,000 people to the east of Nanga-Eboko.

A.73b GBĬGBĬL [Bobili]

Spoken in Cameroun by some 6,000 people on the eastern bank of the R. Long, near the point where it joins the R. Sanaga.

A.74 BULU and BĔNĔ

A.74a BULU

Spoken over a vast area in the southern part of Cameroun, between 10° E. and 13° E. by about 110,000 people. The sub-tribes speaking this language are known by various names, such as Yengono, Yembama, Yelinda, and Zaman.

A.74b BĔNĔ [Bane]

Spoken in Cameroun to the north of the area of the speakers of 74a, in the direction of M'Balmayo and Yaounde, by about 60,000 people.

A.70 YAUNDE-FANG GROUP

A.75 FAŊ [Pangwe]
Spoken over an enormous area of southern Cameroun, Rio Muni, and Gabon, probably by about 200,000 people. The northern variety of this language is sometimes known as Ntum, and the southern as Make.

LINGUISTIC FEATURES
The type language chosen for this group is A.75 Faŋ.

A. Sound Patterns

The majority of the items in these languages have a monosyllabic basis although polysyllables do occur in both stems and radicals. Closed syllables are very common, as in 75, e.g. **akǫ́k** 'stone', **afap** 'wing', and also occur in non-final positions in radicals, e.g. in 75: **-sįmda** 'think'.

The vowels in these languages vary greatly. In 74 there is a series of seven radical vowels, which differs from the simple series in Groups A.20 and A.30 only in the way ə occurs in junction with certain consonants where ɛ occurs with others. In other languages of the group there are varieties of centralized vowels in radical position. The most complicated series of vowels occurs in 75 where a clear difference has to be made between vowels in non-final radical positions and final radical positions.

(a) In non-final radical position there are seven qualities of vowel with no distinction of quantity: a/ę/ə/į/ǫ/ɔ/ų e.g. **-kak** 'fix', **-tsęk** 'cut', **-bə́k** 'hurt', **-dzį́k** 'become burnt', **-kǫk** 'become enough', **-tɔk** 'boil', **-bvų́k** 'break'.

(b) In final radical position there are at least ten distinct vowels, some of which are long and some short: a/a:/ɛ:/ə/į/į:/ǫ/ɔ/ų:/ü, e.g. **-ya** 'surround', **-yá:** 'be angry', **-lɛ́:** 'say', **-və** 'wake', **-bį** 'hoe' **-bį:** 'follow', **-lǫ́** 'bite', **-bɔ:** 'do', **-kų:** 'be used up', **-sü** 'pour'.

There are various types of consonant series throughout the group. Here again the most complicated position is probably found in 75, where in initial position in radicals a consonant with double articulation may occur that has to be distinguished from a similar simple consonant, e.g. ḳ/k as in **-ḳų:** 'fall', **-kų:** 'be used up'; bj/b as in **-bjį:** 'break', **-bį:** 'follow'. The sound represented by 'ɓ' is imploded.

Tone plays an important part in lexical distinctions, e.g. 75: **-yɛ:** 'sing', **-yɛ́:** 'sleep'. Tone-slip is extremely common; examples will be found under the verbal conjugation.

B. Class System

The class system is surprisingly constant throughout the whole group, and the following outline from 75 will serve as a typical description.

Independent Prefixes

Cl.		e.g.	
Cl. 1/2	ɲ-/bə-	nlǫ́ŋ/bəlǫ́ŋ	'builder/builders'
Cl. 3/4	ɲ-/mįɲ-	nlə́m̀/mįnlə́m̀	'heart/hearts'
Cl. 5/6	a-/mə-	alɔ́/məlɔ́	'ear/ears'
Cl. 7/8	ę-/bę-	ękɔn/bękɔn	'banana/bananas'
Cl. 9/6	ɲ-/mən-	ndá/məndá	'house/houses'
Cl. 11/5	ǫ-/a-	ǫkəŋ/akəŋ	'knife/knives'

In vowel junction:

| Cl. 5/6 | dz-/m- | e.g. dzal/mal | 'village/villages' |
| Cl. 7/8 | dz-/bj- | e.g. dzá/bjá | 'song/songs' |

Dependent Prefixes

These mainly have the same shape in 75 as the word 'this': e.g. 1. nyj̣ 2. ba 3. ẅj̣ 4. mj̣ 5. dj̣ 6. mə 7. dzj̣ 8. bj̣ 9. nyj̣ 11. ẅj̣. In certain series however, the prefix of Cl. 1 is ǫ- and Cl. 9, dzj̣-.

C. POSSESSIVES

The possessive stems in these languages are fragmentary and as will be seen from the following list for 75, those for the second and third persons for Cl. 1 are distinguished by tone only in this language.

    Cl. 1. 1st: -ám   2nd: -j̣á   3rd: -ja
    Cl. 2. 1st: -a   2nd: -jna   3rd: -ɔ

D. NUMERALS

There is a simple decimal system of counting throughout the group, '1'-'5' being dependent nominals, and '6'-'9' independent.

E. NOMINAL SENTENCES

It is rare for sentences in these languages to consist of nominals only. The following examples from 75 with a copula -nə are typical of what occurs in the other languages.

    1. ŋkɔl ẅj̣ ǫnə ęyaló   'this rope is long'
    2. mj́ŋkɔl mj́ mj́nə bj̣yaló 'these ropes are long'

F. VERBAL SYSTEM

There is a great similarity in the verbal system of the different languages. The following outline refers to 75, but may be regarded as typical.

Affirmative Conjugation

The following are some of the commoner tenses:

1. Remote Past	-ŋgá¹-	e.g. bj̣ŋgá'yɔ́p	'we fished'
2. Near Past	-váyə́¹-	e.g. bj̣váyə́'yɔ́p	'we fished'
3. Future	-kə-	e.g. bj̣kəyɔ́p	'we shall fish'
4. Aspect of Completion	—	e.g. bj̣yɔ́byə́	'we have fished'
5. Aspect of Progress	-á¹-	e.g. bj̣á'yɔ́p	'we are fishing'
6. Aspect of Repetition	-wú¹-	e.g. bj̣wú'yɔ́p	'we fish'

The rules governing the shape of the base in Tense 4 are complicated. The following examples are typical of the relationship between the simple base used in other tenses and that used in Tense 4: -bɔ:/-bɔŋɔ 'be able', -kụ:/-kpak 'fall', -wǫbə/-wǫbga 'wash', -fɛ:/-fɛyɛ 'choose'.

Negative Conjugation

1. Remote Past	-ɛŋgádj̣á¹-	e.g. bj̣ɛŋgádj̣á'yɔ́p	'we did not fish'
2. Near Past	-ɛváyə́dj̣á¹-	e.g. bj̣ɛváyə́dj̣á'yɔ́p	'we did not fish'

3. Future	-ɛ́- -djá	e.g. bjɛ́'yɔ́bdjá	'we shall not fish'
4. 'Not Yet'	-ábədjá'-	e.g. bjábədjá'yɔ́p	'we have not yet fished'
5. Aspect of Progress	-á'- -djá	e.g. bjá'yɔ́bdjá	'we are not fishing'
6. Aspect of Repetition	-ɛwų́djá'-	e.g. bjɛwų́djá'yɔ́p	'we do not fish'

Reduplicated Radicals

In 75 extra verbal forms occur in Tenses 1–3, both affirmative and negative, distinguished by the presence of a reduplicated first syllable of the radical. These express the aspect of repetition, e.g. Tense 1: bjŋgá'yɔ́yɔ́p 'we used to fish'. In some languages, such as 74, similar forms occur in which the reduplicated first syllable always contains a neutral vowel, e.g. bjŋgáyəyɔ́p.

Personal Prefixes

Cl. 1. 1st: mə-   2nd: ǫ-   3rd: a-
Cl. 2. 1st: bj-   2nd: mj-   3rd: bə-

In other classes the dependent prefix usually has the same shape as the independent prefix, except that in junction with -a- or -ɛ- there is Cl. 5: d-, Cl. 7, 9: dz-.

Object Substitutes

These do not occur in every language, but a number of others have personal O.S. of the same general type as the following list from 75.

Cl. 1. 1st: mə́   2nd: wə́   3rd: nyə́
Cl. 2. 1st: bjə́   2nd: mjnə́ 3rd: bə́

In other classes in 75 the pattern is dependent prefix plus ə́. The position of these substitutes is governed by complicated rules, but in general they occur in a position similar to that shown for the negative element djá; when both elements occur the object substitute follows the negative element. The tonal behaviour of the object substitute is very complicated and without giving a large number of examples it is not possible to illustrate it, although it is partly upon such grounds that the word division of verbals has to be decided.

G. NOMINO-VERBALS

This category does not appear to be applicable in many of the languages of the group, although in 75 there are nomino-verbals of limited use with the prefix ę-, e.g. ęsɛ́: 'to work'.

H. EXTENSIONS

Extended radicals of regular patterns that can be related to simple radicals, are not a characteristic of these languages.

The following type of relationship from 75 is, however, typical of what may be found in most of these languages.

Causative: -ələ e.g. -dzįm/-dzįmələ 'go out/extinguish'
                   -dzɛ:/-dzalə   'become full/fill'

K. ADDITIONAL OBSERVATIONS

Vocabulary Content

At first sight the vocabularies of these languages appear peculiar, but in fact there is a surprisingly large proportion of the items in them which can be shown to be related to those in Bantu languages outside the area.

Sound correspondences

For 71, 72a, and 74 the correspondences of the radical vowels with the starred vowels are straightforward. In 75, however, there are complications, due to the peculiar correspondences with starred stems where the second radical consonant is *d, e.g.:

*-cádá → ęsέ: 'work'
*-bèdè → abj: 'thigh'
*-yúdù → dzű 'nose'

Internal Relationships

The most complex members of the group appear to be 72a and 74. The others all display a measure of reduction, but this is not necessarily of the same kind in each case.

General Affinities

As this group extends over a very large area its members are in juxtaposition with the languages of a number of other groups. They display little affinity with the following of these neighbouring groups; A.20, A. 30, and A. 50, and B.10 and B.20. There is, however, some affinity with A.40 and A. 80. Although many of the characteristics of this group appear to be different from those of the great majority of the Bantu languages, there would appear to be little or no justification for the suggestion that it shows any affinity with non-Bantu languages.

SOURCES

MS. notes on the whole group, except A. 72a and A. 73b.
A.72a: *Die Sprache der Jaunde in Kamerun*, by H. Nekes, 1913.
      Jaunde-Wörterbuch, by M. Heepe, 1926.
A.74a: *Handbook of Bulu*, by G. Bates, 1926.
A.75: *Encyclopédie Pahouine*, by V. Largeau, 1901.

A.80 MAKAA-NJEM GROUP

THE languages of this group are widely scattered, the most westerly occurring along the coastal strip in Cameroun, while others are over on the border between Cameroun and Oubangui-Chari. One member of the group actually occurs in Gabon and Moyen Congo, south of the Cameroun border.

A.81 *MVUMBO* [Ngumba]
Spoken by about 10,000 people in several distinct areas in the West of Cameroun and in the north-west corner of Rio Muni. The most southerly speakers are known as Mabi [Mabea] or Bisiẅo.

A.82 *SO*
Spoken by about 6,000 people in the Akonolinga subdivision of Cameroun.

A.83 *MAKAA*
Spoken by over 40,000 people in an irregular-shaped area with its centre approximately at Abong-Mbang in Cameroun.

A.84 *NJĚM* [Djem, Dzimu]
Spoken in Cameroun by some 20,000 people thinly spread over a vast area of otherwise uninhabited forest country to the south of the Makaa. The speakers of this language include the peoples called Dzimu, Badjue, and Esel. The name Kozime has also been used for this language.

A.85 *KǪNABEM* and *BƐKWIL*

A.85a *KǪNABEM* [Konabembe]
Spoken by about 3,000 people in Cameroun to the south of Yokadouma. The people called Boman also speak this language.

A.85b *BƐKWIL* [Bakwele]
Spoken by about 5,000 people in the districts of Souan Ké and Sembe in Moyen Congo and the Mekambo district of Gabon.

A.86 *MBIMU*

A.86a *MƐDJĮMƐ*
Spoken by about 2,000 people on the south bank of the R. Boumé. The most easterly speakers are known as Bayaatu [Bangando].

A.86b *MPƆ̌MPƆ̌* [Bombo]
Spoken by some 4,000 people just to the west of Yokadouma.

A.86c *MPJƐMƆ* [Mbimu]
Spoken by about 8,000 people astride the boundary between Cameroun and Oubangui-Chari, to the east of Yokadouma.

A.87 BǪMWALĮ

Spoken in Moyen Congo mainly on the south bank of the R. Ngoko and the R. Sanga for about 120 miles downstream from Soufflay. The people along the eastern part of this area are also known as Lino.

LINGUISTIC FEATURES

The type language chosen is A.83 Makaa.

A. Sound Patterns

These languages are mainly monosyllabic and use many closed syllables, e.g. 83: -bwát 'wear', laak 'horn'. There are many more two-syllable stems in 81 and 82, while closed syllables are rare in 82.

In 81 there is a simple series of five radical vowels, but in the remaining languages the vowel qualities are extremely varied and from the available information it is impossible to say exactly how many distinctions of vowel there are in any position. Nasalized vowels and centralized vowels are of frequent occurrence, as in the following examples from 83, -dɔ̃ 'draw water', -tʃĩɛl 'tie', -sɨs 'approach', bɔ̈ɔ̈k 'hoe', -nyä 'tear'. In 81 there is a peculiar sound in final position, mainly in two-syllable words, consisting of a central vowel with constriction of the pharynx and friction of the epiglottis, as for example in zirə 'darkness'.

The incidence of two quantities of vowel varies considerably from language to language, but frequently, as in 83, there are two quantities in both closed and open syllables, e.g. -bát 'go up', -laat 'sew', -dʒį́ 'ask', dʒįį 'cry'.

Imploded voiced stops occur mainly in 85 and 86. The consonants of 84 are very varied and this language is unusual in having a final -h, e.g. djh 'eye'. Initial long consonants occur here and there, as in 82, e.g. ggyo 'tooth', ddu 'nose'.

Tone is an important feature and frequently serves as a lexical distinction, as in 83, e.g. -dʒį́ 'ask', -dʒį 'sit'.

B. Class System

The classes in these languages are fewer in number than those commonly found in Bantu languages. The following list gives all the independent prefixes that have been observed in 83.

Cl. 1/2	mų-/bų-	e.g. mwųdá/bwųdá	'woman/women'
Cl. 3/4	-/mį-	e.g. lám̀/mįlám̀	'heart/hearts'
Cl. 5/6	-/mə-	e.g. lę́/məlę́	'tree/trees'
Cl. 5/8	-/į-	e.g. käla/įkäla	'mat/mats'
Cl. 5/9	-/n-	e.g. bųmá/mpųmá	'fruit/fruits'
Cl. 9/6	n-/mən-	e.g. mpĕ/məmpĕ	'pot/pots'

The use of an identical pattern of agreement in the cases numbered Cl. 5 above is a characteristic of the whole group, except in 82 where there are different classes as the singular of Cl. 6 and Cl. 8. In some cases there are peculiarities in words occurring in Cl. 1/2, e.g. 84: mǫmá/bǫbá 'woman/women', 86: mjá/bǫá 'man/men'.

A.80 MAKAA-NJEM GROUP

Dependent Prefixes

There do not seem to be many series of dependent prefixes. The following list from 83 shows the peculiar nature of some of the agreements.

1. dʒį-   2. ɔ-   3. ẅį-   4. mį-
5. dʒį-   6. mə-   8. yį-   9. nyį-

An extra dependent prefix is attached without a linking vowel, as in 83, e.g. laak ẅįtɔwụ 'horn of the goat'.

C. Possessives

The stems of possessives are frequently very fragmentary and display some peculiar features in their agreements. The following table shows the possessive stems for the three persons of Cl. 1 in three of the classes in 83.

                1st/2nd/3rd
Cl. 5.   dʒɔ̃/gwɔ/dʒįɛ
Cl. 6.   mɔ̃/mwɔ/mɛ
Cl. 9.   ŋwɔ̃/wụɔ/yɛ

In 81 there is the further peculiarity that some of the stems are very similar in shape, as for example in the following words for 'thy/his/theirs' in Cl. 1, 3, or 9, ŋwô/ŋwó/ŋwóó.

D. Numerals

There is a simple decimal system of counting, numerals '1'–'5' being dependent nominals, and '6'–'9' independent nominals, except in 85 where these are dependent nominals of the type '5' plus '1'.

E. Nominal Sentences

In most of the group simple nominal sentences occur, though sometimes as in 83, it is more usual for a copula (in this case -n̂tʃ) to be used, e.g.:

1. kwɔl óga ẅįn̂tʃ gwa   'this rope is long'
2. mįkwɔl mįga mįn̂tʃ gwa 'these ropes are long'

F. Verbal System

The verbal systems vary somewhat from language to language, but are normally characterized by the absence of tense suffixes in affirmative tenses. The conjugation set out below for 83 is fairly typical of what occurs in other cases.

Affirmative Conjugation

1. Remote Past	-aasį̂	e.g. saasį̂bwáḿ	'we bought'
2. Recent Past	-áá-	e.g. sáábwáḿ	'we bought'
3. Future	-ę́báa-	e.g. sę́báabwáḿ	'we shall buy'
4. Aspect of Progress	-ę́-	e.g. sę́bwáḿ	'we are buying'

Negative Conjugation

1. Past	-áá¹- -ə́gɛ	e.g. sáá¹bwámə́gɛ	'we do not buy'
2. Future	-abááyẹ- byɛ	e.g. sabááyẹbwáḿ byɛ	'we shall not buy'
3. Aspect of Progress	-áá¹- -ɛ́	e.g. sáá¹bwámɛ́	'we are not buying'

In 81 there is a feature not observed elsewhere in the group, which is the use of a special negative auxiliary followed by the simple verbal base for the purpose of expressing negation.

Personal Prefixes

The verbal prefixes vary considerably from language to language, but the following list from 83 will serve to show the general pattern that occurs.

Cl. 1.   1st: **ny-**   2nd: **w-**   3rd: **m-**
Cl. 2.   1st: **s-**   2nd: **bį́-**   3rd: **bų́-**

H. EXTENSIONS

Extended radicals of regular patterns are rare in these languages. In 81 for example there are two distinct types of causative extension, **-ele** and **-uɡu**, e.g. **lunde/lundele** 'become full/fill', **wase/wasuɡu** 'swell/cause to swell'. In this language also there is a passive radical characterized by the suffix **-oo**, e.g. **bvi/bvioo** 'hit/be hit'.

In 83 there is a fairly regular causative extension **-al**, e.g. **dʒį́mp/dʒį́mbal** 'be extinguished/extinguish'.

K. ADDITIONAL OBSERVATIONS

Vocabulary Content

There is a very strong resemblance between each of the vocabularies of this widely scattered group, but the monosyllabic nature of many of the stems and radicals makes it difficult to determine exactly what proportion of any of them is common to other Bantu languages outside the group. From the available material it appears that the proportion is very low.

Sound Correspondences

There are a number of very interesting and unusual correspondences in these languages. One peculiarity is that radicals which have no consonant in first position elsewhere, do have a consonant in these languages, e.g.:

81:   -dʒíw-   (← *-yį́b-)   'steal'
85b: -ję́ę́p   (← *-yímb-)   'sing'

Some of the correspondences for radical vowels are unusual, as the following examples will show.

83:   *a → ɔ   e.g. *-tátù → -lɔ́l   '3'
      *i → a   e.g. *-kímà → -kám   'monkey'
85:   *a → ɛ   e.g. *-tátù → -lɛ́l   '3'

In some cases there are peculiar correspondences for suffixed vowels and it is worth noting that the correct name for 81, Mvumbo, is related to its better known name,

Ngumba, by simple rules of sound correspondence between this language and the coastal languages of Groups A.20 and A.30.

In 85 there is an interesting correspondence for C_2 where in the starred form this consists of a nasal compound. The following example is typical of what occurs in this language, *-kándá → káát 'cloth'.

Internal Relationships

There is a very clear difference in complexity between the members of this group, the direction of the reduction being approximately in the order of the numbering, with the exception of A.84 which is probably the most reduced member of all.

General Affinities

This group is unquestionably appropriate for inclusion among Bantu languages, but its affinities with the family as a whole are rather tenuous. These languages display certain relationships with those of nearby groups, but there is none with which this is particularly close. Although the evidence is scanty, it is nevertheless feasible that there are certain affinities with non-Bantu languages, particularly in the more eastern members of the group.

SOURCES

MS. notes on the whole group.
A.86b: A vocabulary of this language, under the name 'Kaka of Salo' appeared in 'Notes sur les Langues des Pygmées de la Sanga', by Dr. Ouzilleau, in *Revue d'Ethnographie et de Sociologie*, Paris, 1911.

A.90 KAKA GROUP

THE languages in this group are all Sub-Bantu. They are marginal in that for the most part they are either on the extreme fringe of the Bantu area, or are actually spoken in enclaves within regions where non-Bantu languages are spoken.

A.91 *KWAKU̧M* [Bakum, Pakum, Akpwakum]
   Spoken by a few thousand people principally in the Doumé subdivision of Cameroun.

A.92 *PǪL* and *PƆMƆ*

   A.92a *PǪL*
   Spoken in Cameroun by about 2,000 people in three small groups in close proximity to A.91.

   A.92b *PƆMƆ*
   Spoken in Oubangui-Chari in a few scattered villages along the east bank of the R. Sanga for about 60 miles below Bayanga.

   A.93 *KAKƆ* [Kaka, Yaka]
   Spoken mainly in the Batouri subdivision of Cameroun, and also across the border in Oubangui-Chari, by about 40,000 people.

LINGUISTIC FEATURES

The type language is A.91 Kwaku̧m.

A. SOUND PATTERNS

Closed syllables are common in each language, e.g. kǫs 'parrot', kǫl 'leg'. Closed syllables also occur in non-final position giving rise to unusual consonant clusters, e.g. sḭktʃḭŋ 'truth', -fḛksa 'try', -dḛŋsɛ 'to fish'.

In radical position there are at least seven vowels. In 91 there are eight radical vowels, but it is unlikely that the sounds occurring as **e**, **ɛ**, and **ə** represent more than two distinctions of vowel quality. In 93 there are nasalized vowels in one-syllable stems, e.g. **tũ** 'house'.

In 91 it is not clear whether there are two quantities of vowel or not, since in each case where a long vowel has been observed there is a similarity in the general pattern of the word, e.g. **laakɔ** 'horn', **nyaamɔ** 'animal', **fáásɔ́** 'twin', **-kaamɛ** 'desire', **-kaawɛ** 'divide'. In 92a on the other hand, long vowels appear to occur quite regularly, both in non-final syllables, e.g. **-bɔ́ɔ́mɔ** 'buy' and in one-syllable stems, e.g. **sḛḛ** 'path'.

Implosive consonants apparently do not occur, but long initial consonants sometimes do, as in 91, e.g. **ggwálá** 'drum', **ttɔ́** 'ear'.

Tone is regularly used, and may serve to express a lexical distinction, e.g. in 91, **bɛ́l** 'breast', **bɛl** 'thigh'. Tone-slip occurs in a number of cases, but appears to be confined to word junctions, as in 91, e.g. **jḭ¹ fɛ́nɛ́** 'it is here'.

B. CLASS SYSTEM

Independent Prefixes

There are fewer distinct classes in the other languages than in 91. In 92a there are

A.90 KAKA GROUP

only six, while in 93 a prefix **bę-** is attached to form the plurals of words referring to persons, and **mɛ-** in other cases.

The prefixes in 91 are numerous and it is difficult to relate them with any certainty to those of other Bantu languages. In the following list therefore the classes have been distinguished by letters rather than by figures.

Cl. A/B	mǫ-/gwǫ-	e.g. mǫmja/gwǫmja	'woman/women'
Cl. C/C	ń-/ń-	e.g. ńjɔ́pu̧/ńjɔ́pu̧	'fishhook/fishhooks'
Cl. C/D	ń-/n-	e.g. m̀baapɔ́/mbaapɔ́	'wing/wings'
Cl. C/E	n-/-	e.g. nkɔku̧/kɔku̧	'stone/stones'
Cl. E/D	-/n-	e.g. sǫ/nsǫ	'tooth/teeth'
Cl. E/E	-/-	e.g. sěl/sěl	'pot/pots'
Cl. E/F	-/j̧	e.g. kəŋ/j̧kəŋ	'well/wells'
Cl. E/K	-/-	e.g. telę/telę	'mat/mats'
Cl. G/H	kj-/j̧-	e.g. kj̧dę/j̧dę	'cloth/cloths'
Cl. K/D	-/n-	e.g. banj̧j̧/mbanj̧j̧	'slap/slaps'
Cl. K/K	-/-	e.g. lɛm/lɛm	'axe/axes'
Cl. L/G	fj̧-/kj̧	e.g. fj̧ɛtj̧/kj̧fj̧ɛtj̧	'tree/trees'

Sometimes a word in Cl. E has a prefix **ę-**, although this is apparently optional, e.g. **tǫ́** or **ętǫ́** 'house'.

Dependent Prefixes

The occurrence of an agreement is very similar in all the languages of the group except that there are few types of agreement other than in 91, while even here dependent prefixes are limited to certain nominal words. They are however regularly used with a stem such as **-nɔ́** 'this'.

A. wu̧-	B. yj̧-	C. wu̧-	D. mj̧-	E. lj̧-
F. yj̧-	G. tʃj̧-	H. lj̧-	K. yj̧-	L. fj̧-

It is interesting to note that in 92a many independent words in the plural have **wu̧-**, which agrees with **bj̧-** in dependent words, whereas in similar words in 92b there is **bj̧-** in both cases.

C. Possessives

The behaviour of possessives in these languages is peculiar in that there is an agreement in some cases but not in others, as may be seen from these examples from 91.

(a) When used with an independent nominal in a two-word sentence the possessive has a regular dependent prefix, e.g. **lj̧ámbɔ́** 'my (Cl. E)', **tʃámbɔ́** 'my (Cl. G)', as **ękę lj̧ámbɔ́** 'it is my egg', **kj̧kəŋ tʃámbɔ́** 'it is my knife'.

(b) When preceded by the element **j̧i** 'it is' there are two forms only, the singular and the plural, independent of the class of the sentence, e.g. **gwámbɔ́** (sing.), **jámbɔ́** (plur.).

ękę lj̧nɔ́ j̧i gwámbɔ́	'this egg is mine'
ŋkę mj̧nɔ́ j̧i jámbɔ́	'these eggs are mine'
kj̧kəŋ tʃj̧nɔ́ j̧i gwámbɔ́	'this knife is mine'
j̧kəŋ yj̧nɔ́ j̧i jámbɔ́	'these knives are mine'

D. Numerals

There is a simple decimal system of counting, but the numerals are all invariable. In 91 '1'–'5' are apparently constructed with a prefix **n-**, while '6'–'9' have no prefix, e.g. ntaan '5', sál '8'.

E. Nominal Sentences

In 91 sentences of the following type normally contain the element **ji**,

1. kɔl wų́nɔ́ ji lawáwę   'this rope is long'
2. kɔl lį́nɔ́ ji lawáwę   'these ropes are long'

The following example from 93 will demonstrate the complexity of sentences in this language. The final element tę appears to be a sign of the end of the sentence in certain cases.

1. kɔl tę́ yɔkɔ́ nɛ̌ sɛwų́nâ tę   'this rope is long'
2. mɛkɔl mɛtę́ maká nɛ̌ sɛwų́nâ tę   'these ropes are long'

F. Verbal System

The verbal system in each of these languages is of the same general type, that is, tenses are constructed with a suffixed element of the type CV or with a simple infix. The following list of tenses is from 91,

Conjugation

1. Remote Past	-mɛ	e.g.	sɛbɔ́ḿmɛ	'we bought'
2. Near Past	-kǫ	e.g.	sɛbɔ́ḿkǫ	'we bought'
3. Immediate Past	-mɛ́-	e.g.	sɛ́mɛ́bɔ́mɔ́	'we have just bought'
4. Immediate Future	-sɔ́-	e.g.	sɛ́sɔ́bɔ́mɔ́	'we are going to buy'
5. Near Future	-wɛ́-	e.g.	sɛ́wɛ́bɔ́mɔ́	'we shall buy'
6. Remote Future	-fɛ́-	e.g.	sɛfɛ́bɔ́mɔ́	'we shall buy'
7. Aspect of Completion	-ji- -ŋ́	e.g.	sɛjibɔ́mɔ́ŋ́	'we have bought'
8. Aspect of Progress	-m-	e.g.	sɛmbɔ́mɔ	'we are buying'

In 93 the final vowel used when there is an infix is apparently a characteristic of the word, e.g. **-balɔ** 'fall', **-dalɛ** 'pull'.

In addition, the suffixed element **-ma** which occurs in past tenses, may occur with a different linking vowel in different cases, e.g.:

-nyɛtɔ/-nyɛtįma   'laugh'
-bɔ́lɔ/-bɔ́lųma   'dance'
-węyɛ/-węyma   'wash'

Negation

There is a negative tense corresponding to each affirmative tense, as for example in 91 where a negative tense is distinguished by the presence of **-wɛɛ-**. This negative element precedes the radical except in Tenses 1 and 2, when it is suffixed to the complete verbal, e.g.

sɛ́sɔ́wɛɛbɔ́mɔ́   'we are not going to buy'
2. sɛbɔ́ḿkǫwɛ́ɛ́   'we did not buy'

A.90 KAKA GROUP

Personal Prefixes

The following details apply to 91, the others in the group have similar general features.

Singular	1st: **nyẹ-**	2nd: **ɔ-**	3rd: **a-**
Plural	1st: **sɛ-**	2nd: **nɛ-**	3rd: **yẹ-**

For non-personal subjects in this language there is usually no prefix to the verbal, in Tenses 4 and 5 however, the appropriate prefix given above for the third person is sometimes used, e.g.:

Tense 3. **kịkəŋ mɛ́já** 'the knife has just got lost'
Tense 3. **ịkəŋ mɛ́já** 'the knives have just got lost'
Tense 4. **kịkəŋ asɔ́já** 'the knife will get lost'
Tense 4. **ịkəŋ yẹsɔ́já** 'the knives will get lost'

Object Substitutes

There do not appear to be special elements for this purpose. In 91 there is a suffix **-ja** which is used as a substitute for a plural object, e.g. **sɛ́wɛ́bɔ́mɔ́ ịkəŋ** 'we shall buy knives', **sɛ́wɛ́bɔ́mja** 'we shall buy them'.

H. EXTENSIONS

There are few extensions obeying regular rules in these languages. The following example from 91 is typical of those that have been observed.

Causative: **-sɛ** e.g. **-jǫ́mǫ/-jǫ́msɛ** 'become dry/dry'
-tǫ́ndɛ/-tǫ́ŋsɛ 'become full/fill'

K. ADDITIONAL OBSERVATIONS

Vocabulary Content

There are many items common to the languages of this group that are also peculiar to it. The proportion of the vocabularies that is related to Bantu languages elsewhere is rather small.

Sound Correspondences

The following correspondence from 91 is characteristic.

*p → f e.g. *-pód- → -fɔ́l- 'become cold'
*-pít- → -fẹ́t- 'pass'

There is an interesting correspondence for suffix vowels throughout the whole group, illustrated by the following example from 91.

*-a → -ɔ e.g. *-bídá → bẹ́lɔ́ 'pit'
*-túúbá → tǫ́wɔ́ '6'

The true name of 93, Kakɔ, is an illustration of this, the word appearing as Kaka in languages outside the group.

Internal Relationships

The most interesting feature of this group is a very close relationship between the languages numbered 92a and 92b which are spoken about 200 miles apart. The whole group is Sub-Bantu and so it is difficult to apply the description of complexity, although as will be seen from the linguistic description, 91 is clearly more complex than the others.

General Affinities

There is a strong Bantu substratum throughout the whole group, but there may well be much in these languages that has affinity with the surrounding non-Bantu languages. In so far as they are related to other Bantu languages they probably have some affinity with group A.80.

SOURCES

MS. notes on the whole group.

A.93: The now extinct northernmost variety of this language is illustrated in 'Wörterverzeichniss der Heidensprachen Adamauas', in the *Zeitschrift für Ethnologie*, 1910.

B.10 MYENE CLUSTER

THIS cluster of dialects is spoken by a number of small groups of people in the western part of Gabon. According to former statements they must have been important languages in the past, but now appear to be rapidly becoming extinct.

B.11a *MPǪDGWĘ*
Spoken by about 1,000 people on both sides of the Gabon estuary.

B.11b *RǪDGǪ* [Orungu]
Spoken by nearly 2,000 people round about the Cap Lopez region of the coast.

B.11c *GALWA*
Spoken by about 2,000 people near Lambaréné and around L. Onangué.

B.11d *DYỤMBA* [Adjumba]
Spoken by a small group on the south bank of the R. Ogooué, near Lambaréné.

B.11e *ŊKƆMĮ*
Spoken by about 5,000 people along the coastal belt, north of Setté Cama.

LINGUISTIC FEATURES

The differences between these dialects do not appear to be very great, except in the details of the verbal system. The following outline is based on B.11a Mpǫŋgwę.

A. SOUND PATTERNS

There are no observed cases of closed syllables, but in junction with another word, the final sound of a word may be a consonant, as in 11a, e.g. **ḿbękǫ́lá** 'I shall buy', **įŋgɔ́yį** 'cloths', **ḿbękǫ́l įŋgɔ́yį** 'I shall buy cloths'.

There is a simple series of seven radical vowels, with no distinction of quantity.

The voiced stops are normally imploded in each of the dialects, a fact not indicated in the spelling of the examples.

The most peculiar feature of the consonants of these dialects is that the number of distinctions in certain positions is exactly half the number in other positions. Some details of this feature are given at the end of the list of independent prefixes.

Some unusual nasal sounds occur in these dialects, for example there is an alveolar nasal sound, written **ṉ**, which is distinct from simple **n**, e.g. -**ṉwan**- 'wear a loin cloth', -**ṉwan**- 'buy on credit'. There are three such nasal sounds, **m̱**, **ṉ**, and **ṉy**, and their distinctive quality is that the oral closure is not quite complete, while in 11a **m̱** the lips are also slightly rounded. If it were not for their position within the consonant framework, they could be equally well considered as nasalized fricative sounds.

This cluster does not make much use of distinctions of tone for lexical purposes, but as may be seen in the verbal conjugation, tone patterns are extremely important there, while tone-slip is a regular feature.

B. CLASS SYSTEM

The following features of the class system apply to 11a, but the differences in the other dialects are quite small.

Independent Prefixes

Cl. 1/2	o̩-/a-	o̩yɛ́nda/ayɛ́nda	'stranger/strangers'
Cl. 3/4	o̩-/i̩-	o̩tóndo̩/i̩tóndo̩	'basket/baskets'
Cl. 5/6	i̩-/a-	i̩rɛ́ndɛ/arɛ́ndɛ	'thorn/thorns'
Cl. 7/8	e̩-/-	e̩rɛ́mi̩/rɛ́mi̩	'axe/axes'
Cl. 9/10	n-/i̩n-	mbó̩ni̩/i̩mbó̩ni̩	'goat/goats'
Cl. 11/19	o̩-/i̩-	ó̩ru̩e/ítu̩e	'hair/hairs'

In the case of words in the classes numbered 11/19, there are only ten distinctions of initial stem consonant as against a possible twenty in all the other classes. For this purpose the consonants may be assorted into the following pairs, where the first is that appropriate for Cl. 11 and the second that for Cl. 19:

1. β, p   2. r, t   3. ɣ, k   4. w, b   5. l, d
6. y, i̩   7. v, f   8. z, s   9. m̩, m   10. n̩, n

In vowel junction:

Cl. 1/2	o̩ŋw-/aw-	o̩ŋwána/awána	'child/children'
Cl. 3/4	o̩ŋw-/i̩mi̩	o̩ŋwáŋga/i̩mi̩áŋga	'iron/irons'
Cl. 5/6	i̩ny-/am-	i̩nyána/amána	'charcoal (piece/pieces)'

With a bilabial consonant in first stem position:

Cl. 3/4	o̩m-/i̩m-	o̩mbó̩ma/i̩mbó̩ma	'python/pythons'
Cl. 5/6	i̩-/am-	i̩wɛ́ni̩/ambɛ́ni̩	'breast/breasts'
		i̩βáβa/ampáβa	'wing/wings'

Dependent Prefixes

These are identical in Cl. 3 and Cl. 11. There are several series of dependent prefixes of which the following from 11*a* with the stems -ɛnɛ 'other' and -βo̩lo̩ 'big' will serve as an illustration:

Cl. 1. o̩wɛnɛ, o̩mpo̩lo̩	Cl. 2. awɛnɛ, aβo̩lo̩	Cl. 3. o̩wɛnɛ, o̩mpo̩lo̩
Cl. 4. i̩mi̩ɛnɛ, i̩mpo̩lo̩	Cl. 5. i̩nyɛnɛ, i̩βo̩lo̩	Cl. 6. amɛnɛ, ampo̩lo̩
Cl. 7. ezɛnɛ, ebo̩lo̩	Cl. 8. yɛnɛ, βo̩lo̩	Cl. 9. nyɛnɛ, mpo̩lo̩
Cl. 10. si̩nyɛnɛ, si̩po̩lo̩	Cl. 19. si̩i̩ɛnɛ, si̩po̩lo̩	

An extra dependent prefix in 11*a* is attached with -i̩-, e.g. o̩rálo̩ w̩i̩náyo̩ 'floor of the house'.

D. NUMERALS

There is a simple decimal system of counting, '1'–'5' being dependent nominals, and '6'–'9' independent.

E. NOMINAL SENTENCES

These do occur, although frequently a copula is used. The following examples are from 11*c*; the copula is optional and so is put in parentheses.

1. o̩yó̩li̩ w̩i̩nó̩ (w̩i̩rɛ́) o̩lá   'this rope is long'
2. i̩yó̩li̩ i̩nó̩ (yi̩rɛ́) i̩lá   'these ropes are long'

F. VERBAL SYSTEM

The general features of the verbal system are the same throughout the cluster, although the details vary. The following outline refers to 11a.

Affirmative Conjugation

The conjugation is of such a nature that it proves impracticable to abstract the tense signs. The characteristic of a given tense will consist of a suffix (with or without an infix), the use of one of two series of dependent prefixes with one or other member of the pairs of consonants in first stem position, and a given tone pattern, e.g.:

1. Remote Past	e.g.	aγólį	'he bought'
2. Near Past	e.g.	akǫ́lá	'he bought'
3. Future	e.g.	ẹbẹ́'kǫ́lá	'he will buy'
4. Aspect of Completion	e.g.	akǫ́lį	'he has bought'
5. Aspect of Progress	e.g.	ekǫ́'lá	'he is buying'
6. Aspect of Repetition		-aγ-	
(1) Remote Past	e.g.	aγǫ́láγį́	'he used to buy'
(2) Near Past	e.g.	akǫ́láγa	'he has been buying'
(3) Future	e.g.	ẹbẹ́'kǫ́láγá	'he will buy repeatedly'

Negative Conjugation

1. Past	e.g.	ẹkǫ́la	'he did not buy'
2. Future	e.g.	ẹbẹ́kǫ́la	'he will not buy'
3. Aspect of Progress	e.g.	ẹpákǫ́la	'he is not buying'

It will be seen that the only difference between an affirmative and a negative future tense is in the tone pattern used.

Personal Prefixes

In the following list the two types of personal prefix used with the various tenses are separated by a semi-colon:

Cl. 1. 1st **mja-; mj-; m-** 2nd **wa-; ǫ-** 3rd **a-; ẹ-**
Cl. 2. 1st **azwa; azwɛ** 2nd **aṉwa; aṉwɛ** 3rd **ẅa-; ẅj-**

It is debatable whether the forms given for the first and second persons of Cl. 2 are separate words or not, which is why they have been shown without a hyphen. The probability is, however, that they do behave as part of the verbal even though historically they may have been self-standing words.

Relative Constructions

With a subject antecedent special tone patterns are used, which are usually characterized by the presence of a high tone on the first syllable, as in 11a, e.g.:

Affirmative Tense 2: **zį́ nẹ́pέlɛ záju̇'wá** 'this is the plate that got smashed'.

By the use of a passive verbal in similar constructions sentences are formed to express what in other languages would involve the use of an object antecedent, as in 11a, e.g.:

Affirmative Tense 2: **yį́ nįswáka yáγǫ́lǫ njrɛrį-amį** 'this is the knife bought by my father'.

When a personal substitute is used in passive constructions of this kind it is not preceded by an element nị- 'by', but stands alone immediately following the relative verbal, e.g.:

Affirmative Tense 1: wí nótǫ̀ndǫ́ wáɣǫ́lị́ǫ́ mịɛ 'this is the basket bought by me'.

G. NOMINO-VERBALS

These words have a prefixed element ɣǫ-, but it is not certain that this can enter into an agreement, e.g. ɣǫɣǫla 'to buy'.

H. EXTENSIONS

A number of extensions regularly occur in these dialects. In the following examples from 11a the radical is shown in its two different shapes in each case:

Applied: -ịṇ-   e.g. -ɣǫl-,-kǫl-/-ɣǫlịṇ-,-kǫlịṇ-   'buy/buy for'
Causative: -ị-   e.g. -βẹnd-,-pẹnd-/-βẹndị-,-pẹndị- 'become big/make big'
             -ịz-   e.g. -lɛl-,-dɛl-/-lɛlịz-,-dɛlịz-   'become soft/soften'
Reciprocal: -aṇ-   e.g. -wǫl-,-bǫl-/-wǫlaṇ,-bǫlaṇ-   'hit/hit each other'
Reversive: Active/Neuter -ụ-/-ụṇ- e.g. -βụr-,-pụr-/-βụrụ-,-pụrụ-/-βụrụṇ-, -pụrụṇ- 'bind/become unbound/unbind'
Passive: -ǫ   e.g. -ɣǫl-,-kǫl-/-ɣǫlǫ,-kǫlǫ   'buy/be bought'

The passive extension is abnormal in that it follows the suffix -ị and displaces the tense suffix -a, e.g. zaɣǫ́lị́ǫ́ 'it (Cl. 7) was bought'; zịbɛ́'ɣǫ́lǫ́ 'it (Cl. 7) will be bought'.

K. ADDITIONAL OBSERVATIONS

Vocabulary Content

The vocabularies of this cluster have many peculiar items, but also a number related to Bantu languages right outside the area, e.g.:

    ǫmpɛ́nị (← *-pínị) 'handle'
    ịpɔ́kụ   (← *-pòkừ) 'blind person'
    ŋgɔ́rị   (← *-gòtị) 'nape'

Sound Correspondences

These are involved owing to the peculiar nature of the consonant distinctions, but the following is worth noting.

    *d → ṇ e.g. *-búd- → -wụṇ-, -bụṇ- 'become plentiful'
    *-jàdà → nịánạ   'hunger'

General Affinities

Superficially these dialects might appear to be related to A.30 on the one side and B.20 on the other, but in fact they constitute a very distinct isolated language which probably displays as much relationship to Bantu languages elsewhere as to those in the near neighbourhood.

SOURCES

MS. notes on the whole cluster.
B.11a: *Heads of Mpongwe Grammar*, by J. L. Wilson, 1879.

B.20 KELE GROUP

B.21 *SƐKĮYANĮ* [Sheke, Bulu]
   Spoken by an almost extinct tribe on the coast of Gabon, to the north of Libreville.

B.22 *KƐLƐ*
   B.22a *KƐLƐ*, dį-
   Spoken by a very small group on the estuary of the Gabon.
   B.22b *KƐLƐ*, a- or dį, or *ƊGƆM*, a- [Bangomo]
   Spoken in Gabon by a number of scattered groups of people totalling about 11,000, one on the southern bank of the R. Ogooué between N'Djolé and Booué, another to the east of Sindara, a third in the region of Koulamotou, and a fourth far to the north-east in the neighbourhood of Mekambo.
   B.22c *BŲBĮ*
   Spoken in Gabon by about 4,000 people to the west of Koulamotou.

B.23 *MBAƊWƐ*
   Spoken in Moyen Congo by about 2,000 people to the west of Franceville.

B.24 *WŲMBVŲ*
   Spoken in Gabon by about 4,000 people to the east of Ndendé.

B.25 *KǪTA*, į- [Shake, Mahongwe]
   This language is spoken by a tribe numbering about 28,000 people, whose main area is in the region bounded by the rivers Livindo and Upper Ogooué, mainly in Gabon, but also across the boundary into Moyen Congo. Further groups occur in Moyen Congo as far separated as just to the south of Ouesso, and in the region of Ombaïa and Sibiti.

LINGUISTIC FEATURES

The type language is B.22b Kɛlɛ (Ngɔm).

A. SOUND PATTERNS

The patterns of 22b are very complicated and it is doubtful whether the term syllable is really of much value in describing it. Many words end in consonants when in final position, e.g. **mábɛð** 'milk' or **anzụd** 'lion'. Final consonants are rarer in the other languages.

One peculiarity of 22b is that a word in final position may be much longer than a comparable word in close relationship with what follows, e.g. **anɔɔŋụ/bęnɔɔŋụ** 'bed/beds', **bęnɔɔ bęnɛn** 'big beds'.

There is a series of seven radical vowels in each language, but in 22b centralized vowels frequently occur in other positions, e.g. **apɛpɔ̈kɛ̈** 'wing'. There is a peculiar sound in prefix position in most of these languages, which consists of a kind of syllabic nasalized semivowel in which the top teeth are almost in contact with the inside of the bottom lip, as in 25, ꬰhjŋga 'rope'.

The voiced stops of these languages are normally imploded.

There are a number of interesting consonant sounds in these languages. These include in 22b a voiced dental fricative ð, an implosive 'ɗ' and a flapped 'ɽ'. In 22a there are long initial consonants, as in ssɛ́ 'fish'. One feature of the whole group is the occurrence of consonants with the additional articulation of contact between the top teeth and the inside of the bottom lip, as in 22b, e.g. ḓḓu̱/m̱m̱u̱ 'fire/fires'.

The tone patterns of these languages are rather complicated. In 22a rising and falling tones are particularly frequent in context, e.g. **pa nyḭ nyḭyḭ nyḭbɛŋ** (\ ∨ / / ⁻ \) 'the knife is good'.

B. Class System

Independent Prefixes

The following list refers to 22b.

Cl.		e.g.	
Cl. 1/2	ꬰ-/ba-	ꬰðɛŋ/baðɛŋ	'stranger/strangers'
Cl. 3/4	ꬰ-/me̱-	ꬰʃíŋ/me̱ʃíŋ	'rope/ropes'
Cl. 5/6	rë-/ma-	rěkaŋga/mákaŋga	'hoe/hoes'
Cl. 7/8	a-/be̱-	ákaŋ/bé̱kaŋ	'garden/gardens'
Cl. 9/6	n-/man-	mbó̱ka/mambó̱ka	'village/villages'
Cl. 11/10	ða-/n-	ðáwɔkwɛ/mpɔ́kwɛ	'broom/brooms'
Cl. 14	u̱-	u̱djɽu̱	'weight'
Cl. 19/13	yḭ-/ɽa-	yḭnɔ́nɛ/ɽanɔ́nɛ	'bird/birds'

In vowel junction:

Cl.		e.g.	
Cl. 1/2	mw-/ba-	mwán/báán	'child/children'
Cl. 3/4	gw-/mḭ-	gwana/mḭana	'mouth/mouths'
Cl. 5/6	dj-/ma-	djáke̱/mááke̱	'egg/eggs'
Cl. 7/8	gi-/bḭ-	gio̱ŋo̱/bḭo̱ŋo̱	'waterpot/waterpots'
Cl. 14/6	bḭ-/ma-	bḭaɽu̱/máaɽu̱	'canoe/canoes'

In 21 and 24 the prefix of Cl. 6 is mɛ- and that of Cl. 7 is zero. In 22a there is no distinct class to be numbered 14, the prefix and agreements of Cl. 8 occurring where the other languages have Cl. 14, e.g. **bḭsɔ́pɔ́/masɔ́pɔ́** 'land/lands'. In this language also Cl. 19 has the peculiar prefix u̱-, e.g. **u̱nɔnḭ/lanɔnḭ** 'bird/birds'. The Cl. 2a prefix in 24 is bɛ-, e.g. **bɛ́tâta** 'fathers'. In 25 there are a number of words in Cl. 3 with a plural in Cl. 2, e.g. **ntʃeḭ/batʃeḭ** 'stranger/strangers'.

Dependent Prefixes

There are not many different series of dependent prefixes in these languages and the total number of different shapes is further reduced by the fact that frequently certain pairs are identical, for example in 22b, with the stem -nɛn 'big' there are,

Cl. 4 and Cl. 14	e.g. wu̱nɛn
Cl. 7 and Cl. 19	e.g. yḭnɛn
Cl. 9 and Cl. 10	e.g. nyḭnɛn

An extra dependent prefix is attached with no linking element, as in 22b, e.g. **be̱tọ̆bǎ bé̱mwan** 'clothes of the child'.

D. NUMERALS

There is a simple decimal system of counting throughout the group. The numerals '1'–'9' in 22b consist of dependent nominals, '6'–'9' being of the pattern '5' plus '1'. In the other languages the behaviour of the numerals '6'–'9' varies, for example in 25 they are all independent nominals, while in 24 only '6' and '8' are distinct words.

E. NOMINAL SENTENCES

These regularly occur in 25 only. The other languages use a copula of some kind as in the following type of sentences. These are from 22a.

1. gyẹ́rẹ yĭ̧ ĭ̧yĭ̧ yínɛn   'this tree is big'
2. bẹ́ẹ́rẹ bệ bḝyĭ̧ bẹ́nɛn   'these trees are big'

F. VERBAL SYSTEM

The verbal systems vary somewhat throughout the group, the most interesting being in 22b, which is illustrated in the following notes.

Affirmative Conjugation

1. Past	-ẹ	e.g. ánɔtẹ	'he drank'
2. Future	-kẹ-	e.g. ákẹnɔt	'he will drink'
3. Aspect of Completion	-mɛ	e.g. anɔtə́mɛ	'he has drunk'
4. Aspect of Progress	—	e.g. anɔt	'he is drinking'
	-ŋgẹ-	e.g. aŋgẹnɔt	

The suffixes shown for Tenses 1 and 3 are applicable only in the case of certain radicals. In other cases the relationship between the bases in these tenses is much more complicated. Illustrations of this will be found below under the heading Nomino-Verbals.

Negative Conjugation

1. Past	-tẹ- -ẹ	e.g. atẹnɔtẹ	'he did not drink'
2. Future	-tẹ-	e.g. atẹnɔt	'he will not drink'
3. Aspect of Progress	-sa-	e.g. asanɔt	'he is not drinking'

In 25 there is a case where the only difference between an affirmative and the corresponding negative tense is in the tone patterns.

mahɔ́mbáná nyẹtẹ   'I bought bananas'
mă'hɔ́mbáná nyẹtẹ   'I did not buy bananas'

Personal Prefixes

There are distinct forms for the first and second person in Cl. 1 only, in each of the languages 21–24, as in the following list from 22b.

Cl. 1.   1st: **mɛ-**   2nd: **wɛ-**   3rd: **a-**
Cl. 2.   **ba-**

In 25 the difference in the prefixes for the other persons of Cl. 2 is obscured in all except one affirmative tense.

Object Substitutes

These are distinct words, formed in 22*b* on the general pattern, dependent prefix plus -ɔ, for example Cl. 4, **mjɔ**. The following are the forms for Cl. 1 and Cl. 2.

    Cl. 1. 1st: **mɛ** 2nd: **wɛ** 3rd: **yɛ**
    Cl. 2. 1st: **bɛʃɛ** 2nd: **bɛwɛ** 3rd: **bɔ**

Relative Constructions

With an antecedent object there is in 25 a construction in which the subject of the relative verbal is preceded by an element consisting of a dependent prefix agreeing with the antecedent, and the vowel -a, e.g.:

  ŋkándá mwá mwána ahǫ́mbá 'the cloth which the child bought'

G. NOMINO-VERBALS

Nomino-verbals in 22*b* are in Cl. 14, but are frequently characterized also by the use of a special suffixed element, although in certain cases the relationship between this base and those for Affirmative Tenses 1 and 3 is obscure. The following examples illustrate some of the patterns that regularly occur.

    Aff. 1 / *Aff.* 3 / *Nom.-Verb.*
    -nɔtę/-nɔtəmɛ/-nɔtək 'drink'
    -bǫðę/-bǫmɛ/-bǫk 'break'
    -bapyɛ/-bapjmɛ/-bapəky 'carry'
    -wɔręðę/-wɔrəmɛ/-wɔrɛðɔ 'wring'
    -bata/-batamɛ/-batan 'mix'

In 25 there are nomino-verbals in Cl. 5 or Cl. 7 according to the type of context in which they occur.

H. EXTENSIONS

It is difficult to illustrate adequately the relationship between extended radicals and simple radicals but the following two examples from 22*b* given in the form of nomino-verbals will show the kind of thing that occurs in that language.

  Causative: **-ęs- -y** **ų́dųsək/ų́dųsęsəky** 'go out/put out'
  Reciprocal: **-an-** **ų́bjk/ų́bjdyan** 'hit/hit one another'

In 25 the formation of extended radicals may be illustrated by the two following examples of a causative extension, which requires a different suffix from that used with the simple radical.

    -bɔtɔ/-bɔʃję 'go out/extinguish'
    -lǫnda/-lǫʒję 'become full/fill'

K. ADDITIONAL OBSERVATIONS

Vocabulary Content

There is a high proportion of the vocabularies of this group common to it, but much of this is related to what occurs in languages of other groups nearby. There are few items related to Bantu languages elsewhere which are found in this area only in Group B.20.

Sound Correspondences

The most interesting correspondences in these languages are those involving *t and *d in first position, as the following examples will show.

B.21:	*t → t	e.g. *-tádì → dìtádì	'rock'
	*d → d	e.g. *-dímì → dìdémì	'tongue'
B.22a:	*t → l	e.g. *-tímà → nléma	'heart'
	*d → r	e.g. *-dimi → dìrèmì	'tongue'
B.22b:	*t → ṭ	e.g. *-tábì → áṭab	'branch'
	*d → ð	e.g. *-dìdù → ðŏèð	'boundary'
B.24:	*t → ṭ	e.g. *-tímà → ə̃ṭéma	'heart'
	*d → l	e.g. *-dóbò → jìlɔbɔ	'fishhook'

Internal Relationships

There is not much difference in the complexity of these languages, although 22b does display some reduction against 21 and 25.

General Affinities

Apart from vocabulary content which would tend to relate these languages to those of Groups B.40, B.50, and B.60, there is not very marked affinity between them and those of adjacent groups. The relationship of this group to the Bantu languages in general is very clear, but not extensive.

SOURCES

MS. notes on the whole group, except B.22c and B.23.
B.22b: *Grammar of the Bakele Language*, by Preston and Best, 1854.

B.30 TSOGO GROUP

B.31 *TSƆGƆ*, γẹ- [Mitsogo, Apindji]
Spoken in Gabon to the north-east of Mouila for some 50 miles from the R. N'Gougnié.

B.32 *KANDE* [Okande]
This is an almost extinct language spoken in Gabon near Booué, which from the available material would seem to be closely related to 31.

LINGUISTIC FEATURES

The whole of the following outline refers to B.31 Tsɔgɔ.

A. SOUND PATTERNS

There are no closed syllables or final syllabic nasals commonly occurring in this language.

There is a simple series of seven radical vowels, with no distinction of quantity. Occasionally a vowel is pronounced with a centralized quality, e.g. këma 'monkey'.

Among the voiced consonants there are fricative β and γ, while the sounds represented by b and d in the examples are always implosive.

The tone patterns of this language are rather obscure, tone rarely serving to distinguish units.

B. CLASS SYSTEM

Independent Prefixes

Cl. 1/2	mọ-/a-	e.g. moyɛnda/ayɛnda	'stranger/strangers'
Cl. 3/4	mọ-/mị-	e.g. mọ́tẹma/mị́tẹma	'heart/hearts'
Cl. 5/6	ẹ-/ma-	e.g. ẹ́bɔŋgɔ/mábɔŋgɔ	'knee/knees'
Cl. 7/8	γẹ-/ẹ-	e.g. γẹ́tẹtẹ/ẹ́tẹtẹ	'tree/trees'
Cl. 9/10	n-/n-	e.g. mbọ́ma/mbọ́ma	'chest/chests'
Cl. 11/10	ọ-/n-	e.g. ọ́sộγẹ/tsộγẹ	'hair/hairs'
Cl. 11/10a	ọ-/dị-	e.g. ọbọŋgẹ/dịbọŋgẹ	'cloud/clouds'
Cl. 16	βa-	e.g. βámwânza	'on the roof'
Cl. 17	γọ-	e.g. γọ́mbọka	'at the village'
Cl. 19/13	βị-/tọ-	e.g. βị́tẹtẹ/tọ́tẹtẹ	'bush/bushes'

In vowel junction:

Cl. 5/6	-/m-	e.g. ị́nọ/mị́nọ	'tooth/teeth'
Cl. 7/8	s-/ẹ-	e.g. sɔ́tɔ/ẹ́ɔtɔ	'fire/fires'
Cl. 11/10	-/gγ-	e.g. ɛ́ba/gγɛ́ba	'house/houses'
Cl. 17	ọ-	e.g. ọ́ɛba	'at the house'

B.30 TSOGO GROUP

Dependent Prefixes

These are similar to the independent prefixes except that in Cl. 9 there is ẹ-, while Cl. 10 and Cl. 10a have dị- followed by the consonant sound characteristic of Cl. 9, e.g. -bọ̈nị 'small', Cl. 10 and Cl. 10a, e.g. dịpọ̈nị.

An extra dependent prefix is linked with -a-, e.g. mịkọndọ myataba 'tails of the goats'.

D. NUMERALS

There is a simple decimal system of counting, '1'–'5' being dependent nominals, and '9' of the pattern '5' plus '4', while '6'–'8' are independent.

E. NOMINAL SENTENCES

These regularly occur in this language, e.g.:

1. ɛbá ọ́dọ̌ ọɣέọ́ɣɛ   'this house is small'
2. ǵyɛbá ǵyɛ́dị̌ dịkɛ́dịkɛ 'these houses are small'

F. VERBAL SYSTEM

Affirmative Conjugation

1. Remote Past	-ma-	-a	e.g. tọmasọmbá	'we bought'
2. Near Past		-ị	e.g. tọsọmbí	'we bought'
3. Future	-ŋga-	-a	e.g. tọŋgásọmbá	'we shall buy'
4. Aspect of Progress		-a	e.g. tọsọmbá	'we are buying'

Negative Conjugation

1. Remote Past	-sị-	-ẹ	e.g. tọsịsọ́mbẹ́	'we did not buy'
2. Near Past	-sị-	-a	e.g. tọsịsọ́mba	'we did not buy'
3. Future	-saŋga-	-a	e.g. tọsaŋgásọmba	'we shall not buy'
4. Aspect of Progress	-sa-	-a	e.g. tọsásọmba	'we are not buying'

Personal Prefixes

Cl. 1. 1st: na-, n-   2nd: ọ-   3rd: a-
Cl. 2. 1st: tọ-   2nd: nọ- 3rd: a-

G. NOMINO-VERBALS

These are in Cl. 5, e.g. ẹ́sọmba 'to buy'.

H. EXTENSIONS

The following extensions regularly occur.

Applied:	-ẹ-	e.g. -sọmb-/-sọmbẹ-	'buy/buy for'
Causative:	-ẹd-	e.g. -sọmb-/-sọmbẹd-	'buy/sell'
Reciprocal:	-an-	e.g. -bụt-/-bụtan-	'seek/seek one another'
Neuter:	-am-	e.g. -kịt-/-kịtam-	'cut/become cut'
Passive:	-ụ	e.g. -bọt-/-bọtụ	'bear/be born'

K. ADDITIONAL OBSERVATIONS

Vocabulary Content

The vocabulary of B.31 contains many items that are common to the languages of Zone C, but not to the adjacent Zone B languages.

Sound Correspondences

The following correspondences from B.31 are some of the more interesting that occur.

*p → β	e.g. *-pácà → ɛ́βasa	'twin'
*t → t	e.g. *-tábì → mótabẹ	'branch'
*d → zero	e.g. *-da → mọa	'intestine'
*k → ɣ	e.g. *-kádà → máɣaa	'charcoal'
*ġ → k	e.g. *-ġòŋgó → ɛ́kɔŋgɔ	'spear'

General Affinities

This language is definitely more closely related to those far to the east, than to its immediate neighbours. It displays a higher affinity with the more normal type of Bantu language than do most others in Zone B.

SOURCES

MS. notes on B.31.
B.31: *Essai de Grammaire Tsogo*, by A. Walker, 1950.

B.40 SHIRA-PUNU GROUP

B.41 *SIRA*, i- [Shira]
Spoken by about 17,000 people in Gabon for some 50 miles to the south-west of the R. N'Gougnié, between Fougamou and Mouila.

B.42 *SAƉGU*, yi- [Shango]
Spoken by about 18,000 people on Gabon in a narrow belt to the north-east and south-west of Mimongo.

B.43 *PUNU*, yi-
Spoken by about 46,000 people over a large area on both sides of the boundary between Gabon and Moyen Congo, just inland from the coastal plain.

B.44 *LUMBU*, i-
Spoken by about 12,000 people on the coastal plain on both sides of the boundary between Gabon and Moyen Congo.

LINGUISTIC FEATURES

The type language is B.43 Punu.

A. SOUND PATTERNS

There are no closed syllables or final syllabic nasals commonly occurring in these languages.

There is a simple series of five radical vowels in each language. There are also two quantities of radical vowel even before consonants consisting of a nasal compound. In final position in 43, three qualities of vowel only have to be distinguished in words of all kinds, a/i/u. In pre-radical position centralized vowels often occur, e.g. 41: **batsĕdíánzá** 'they worked'.

The consonants in these languages are relatively simple, the voiced stops being implosive, while there are also fricative sounds such as ɣ in each language and β in 41–43.

The tones of the languages of this group are complicated, although there are only two distinct levels, with both rising and falling tones commonly occurring. Since the tone patterns of nominals vary according to their syntactical relationships, no tones are marked on the single words given below.

B. CLASS SYSTEM

The following outline refers to 43, but the class systems of the other languages vary only slightly.

Independent Prefixes

    Cl. 1/2   **mu-/ba-**   e.g. **musalitsi/basalitsi**   'workman/workmen'
    Cl. 3/4   **mu-/mi-**   e.g. **mukudu/mikudu**   'rope/ropes'
    Cl. 5/6   **di-/ma-**   e.g. **dibaɣa/mabaɣa**   'knife/knives'

Cl. 7/8	yi-/bi-	e.g. yibaɣa/bibaɣa	'wall/walls'
Cl. 9/6	n-/man-	e.g. ndaɣu/mandaɣu	'house/houses'
Cl. 11/10	du-/n-	e.g. dulimi/ndimi	'tongue/tongues'
Cl. 14	bu-	e.g. burobu	'mud'
Cl. 16	βa-	e.g. βayikadi	'on the bridge'
Cl. 17	o-	e.g. ondzila	'at the path'

The Cl. 17 prefix is **xu-** in 41, **u-** in 42, and **o-** in 44.

Dependent Prefixes

These are for the most part identical with the independent prefixes. An exception is that for Cl. 3 which is **wu-** in each language.

An extra dependent prefix normally occurs with no linking vowel, as in 43, e.g. **bikútŭ bímwâna** 'clothes of the children'.

D. NUMERALS

There is a simple decimal system of counting, '1'–'6' being dependent nominals, but '7'–'9' independent. In 41 however '7' is expressed by '4' and '3'.

Numerals that are independent nominals usually precede the word they accompany, which is then brought into agreement with them by means of an extra dependent prefix, e.g. 44: **ifú imamányi** '9 stones'.

E. NOMINAL SENTENCES

These regularly occur in each language, the following examples from 43 being typical.

    1. **mwíri éewúwŭ wúneni**   'this tree is big'
    2. **mííri míemímĭ míneni**   'these trees are big'

F. VERBAL SYSTEM

The verbal systems of these languages are of the same general pattern, the following outline from 43 can therefore be taken as typical.

Affirmative Conjugation

1. Remote Past	-ma-	-a	e.g. túmaruuŋgă	'we built'
2. Near Past	-tʃi-	-a	e.g. tútʃíruuŋgă	'we built'
3. Future	—	-a	e.g. túurúuŋgă	'we shall build'
4. Aspect of Completion	-ma-	-a	e.g. tumáruuŋgă	'we have built'
5. Aspect of Progress	-i-	-i	e.g. túirúuŋgĭ	'we are building'

The tones of the tense sign are not given since these vary according to the tone and shape of the radical.

Negative Conjugation

1. Remote Past	-sama-	-a	e.g. tusámaruuŋgă	'we did not build'
2. Near Past	-ɣa-	-a	e.g. tuɣáruuŋgă	'we did not build'
3. Future	-ɣoo-	-a	e.g. tuɣóóruuŋgă	'we shall not build'
4. Aspect of Progress	-ɣee-	-i	e.g. tuɣééruuŋgĭ	'we are not building'

Personal Prefixes

The following typical list is from 43.

    Cl. 1. 1st: **nyi-** 2nd: **u-** 3rd: **a-**
    Cl. 2. 1st: **tu-** 2nd: **du-** 3rd: **ba-**

G. NOMINO-VERBALS

There are words in each language with an affix **u-**, but these do not appear to be able to enter into an agreement. Other nomino-verbal words occur in Cl. 9, e.g. 44: **ntuuŋgulu** 'to build'.

H. EXTENSIONS

The use of extensions in these languages is very regular. The following examples from 43 being typical.

    Applied: **-il-** e.g. **-suumb-/-suumbil-** 'buy/buy for'
    Causative: **-is-** e.g. **-suumb-/-suumbis-** 'buy/sell'
    Neuter: **-iɣ-** e.g. **-ruuŋg/-ruuŋgiɣ-** 'build/become built'

K. ADDITIONAL OBSERVATIONS

Vocabulary Content

The vocabularies of this group contain many items related to those of the adjacent B.50 languages and some that are common to Group H.10.

Sound Correspondences

These contain few features that are very striking and the following four examples from 44 will serve to illustrate the general type of sound correspondence.

    *p → v e.g. *-páŋg- → -vaŋg- 'make'
    *t → r e.g. *-tí → muri 'tree'
    *k → ɣ e.g. *-kín- → -ɣin- 'dance'
    *g → k e.g. *-gàŋg- → -kaŋg- 'tie up'

Internal Relationships

There is a notable uniformity in the complexity of the languages of this group.

General Affinity

These languages show a close relationship with those of Group B.50, and although it is not easy to demonstrate, there would appear to be certain affinities with languages farther to the east.

                  SOURCES

MS. notes on the whole group.

B.50 NJABI GROUP

B.51 *DUMA*, lį-

Spoken by about 10,000 people to the north of the R. Ogooué, round about Lastourville, in Gabon.

B.52 *NZƐBJ*, yį- [Njabi]

Spoken by about 60,000 people over a large area on both sides of the boundary between Gabon and Moyen Congo, astride the second parallel south.

B.53 *TSAADGI*, i-

Spoken by about 15,000 people on both sides of the boundary between Gabon and Moyen Congo, around and to the north of Mossendjo.

LINGUISTIC FEATURES

The type language is B.52 Nzɛbį.

A. Sound Patterns

In final position in 52 closed syllables are common, e.g. **tab** 'goat', although similar words in non-final position may end with **-ə**, e.g. **tabə wúụnų̂w** 'this goat'. This does not appear to happen in the other languages.

There is a simple series of seven radical vowels with a distinction of quantity in 51 and 52, but five radical vowels only in 53. The distinction of quantity occurs also before nasal compounds, e.g. 52: **mįkɔɔŋg** 'hills', **makɔŋg** 'spears'. In final word position in 52 there are two distinctions of vowel only, **-į** and another. This second vowel occurs as **-ə** in current speech, but is similar to a preceeding **u**, **ɛ**, or **ɔ** in deliberate speech, e.g. **matsųųŋg** 'months', **matsųųŋgį máanə̂m** 'these months', **batsųųŋg** 'antelopes', **batsųųŋgə** (or **batsųųŋgų**) **báanə̂b** 'these antelopes'. Each of these two final vowels is unrealized at the end of an utterance, in this position they are therefore indistinguishable, in the examples given below, however, the former is represented by **-į**, while the latter is omitted, except in listing the tense-signs.

The consonants of these languages are not complicated, those represented by **b** and **d** in the examples being implosive.

The rules governing the tone patterns of 52 and 53 are very complicated, so that it is impossible to give the tones of isolated nominals.

B. Class System

The following outline refers to 52.

Independent Prefixes

Cl. 1/2	mų-/ba-	e.g. mųkaas/bakaas	'woman/women'
Cl. 3/4	mų-/mį-	e.g. mųtįįŋgį/mįtįįŋgį	'bottle/bottles'
Cl. 5/6	lə-/ma-	e.g. ləkẹyį/makẹyį	'egg/eggs'
Cl. 7/8	yį-/bį-	e.g. yįsal/bįsal	'work/jobs'

B.50 NJABI GROUP

Cl. 9/6	n-/man-	e.g. nzɛlị/manzɛlị	'river/rivers'
Cl. 14	bụ-	e.g. bụŋgụdị	'strength'
Cl. 5/9	lə-/n-	e.g. ləβend/pend	'groundnut/groundnuts'
Cl. 15	ụ-	e.g. ụkịl	'ironing'
Cl. 16	βa-	e.g. βayịkad	'on the bridge'
Cl. 17	xụ-	e.g. xụmịtị	'by the trees'

In vowel junction:

Cl. 5/6	tsị-/ma-	e.g. tsịamb/maamb	'affair/affairs'
	dị-/mị-	e.g. dịịn/mịịn	'name/names'
Cl. 7/8	sị-/bị-	e.g. sịɛb/bịɛb	'basket/baskets'

The main difference in 51 and 53 is that Cl. 5 and Cl. 11 both have lị- (li-) while Cl. 7 has ẹ- (i-).

Dependent Prefixes

There are two main series in 52, one of which is identical with the independent prefixes, the other is different in one or two classes, e.g. Cl. 3 wụ-, Cl. 7 sị-. Certain stems take a double dependent prefix, e.g. Cl. 3/4 wụmụla/mịmịla 'long'.

An extra dependent prefix is linked with -a-, e.g. 52: yịtakə sịámụtị 'branch of a tree'.

D. NUMERALS

There is a simple decimal system of counting, '1'–'6' being dependent nominals and '7'–'9' independent.

E. NOMINAL SENTENCES

These regularly occur, as in these examples from 52.
1. mụtị wúụnúwǒ wúmụnɛn   'this tree is big'
2. mịtị míịnímǐ mímịnɛn   'these trees are big'

F. VERBAL SYSTEM

The verbal system of 51 is somewhat simpler than that of 52 and 53, but is otherwise of the same general type.

Affirmative Conjugation

The following is a list of the commoner tenses in 52, the final vowel shown as -ə in the tense-signs being realized in speech according to the rules noted above in Section A.

1. General Past	-ama-	-ə	e.g. lámasal	'we worked'
2. Remote Past	-a-	-ə	e.g. lásal	'we worked'
3. Recent Past	-a-	-ị	e.g. lasélị	'we worked'
4. Near Past	-	-ịŋgị	e.g. lə́sɛlịŋgị	'we worked'
5. Immediate Past	-	-ị	e.g. lə́sɛlị	'we have just worked'
6. Immediate Future	-	-ə	e.g. ləsál	'we are going to work'
7. General Future	-ka-	-ə	e.g. ləkasál	'we shall work'
8. Aspect of Completion	-ma-	-ə	e.g. ləmásál	'we have worked'
9. Aspect of Progress	-aa-	-ə	e.g. laasál	'we are working'
10. Aspect of Repetition	-aa-	-əŋgə	e.g. laasáləŋ	'we usually work'

Negative Conjugation

The following are the principal negative tenses in 52. In every case the element βɛ is used at the end of the sentence.

1. General Past   -sa-   -ə   e.g. lə́sasál   'we did not work'
2. Recent Past   -sa-   -į   e.g. ləsasɛ́li   'we did not work'
3. Immediate Past   -sa-   -įŋgį e.g. ləsasɛ́lįŋgį   'we have not worked'
4. Future   -saka- -ə   e.g. ləsakasál   'we shall not work'
5. Aspect of Progress -sa- -ə   e.g. ləsasál   'we are not working'

In 51 and 53 there are no negative tenses, but negation is expressed by prefixing **ka-** to the verbal and placing βɛ (βe) at the end of the sentence, as in 51, e.g.:

lįmálámba nyama   'we cooked meat'
kalįmálámba nyama βɛ   'we did not cook meat'

Personal Prefixes

Cl. 1. 1st: **mɛ-**   2nd: **wɛ-**   3rd: **a-**
Cl. 2. 1st: **lə-**   2nd: **lə-**   3rd: **ba-**

The prefixes for the first and second person of Cl. 1 in 52 are peculiar. They are the same shape for Tenses 1–8 and have a long vowel in 9 and 10, e.g. Tense 2 **mɛ́sal** 'I worked', Tense 9 **mɛɛsál** 'I am working'. In a tense not given in the list, distinguished by an element **nj-** placed before the dependent prefix, e.g. **nįləsál** 'we will (work)', these two prefixes are anomalous in preceding the element, e.g. **mɛnįsál** 'I will (work)'. No doubt these elements were derived from separate personal substitutes, but these also exist and can be added for emphasis, e.g. **mɛ ló mɛɛsál** 'I am working today'.

G. Nomino-Verbals

These are in Cl. 7 in 51, e.g. **ękǫ́ta** 'to tie', and in Cl. 15 in 52 and 53, e.g. 52: **ųxad** 'to tie'.

H. Extensions

Extensions regularly occur in these languages, the following examples from 52 being typical.

Applied: -əl-   e.g. -yǫx-/-yǫxəl-   'hear/obey'
Causative: -əs-   e.g. -rax-/-raxəs-   'fall/drop'
Reversive: -əx-   e.g. -bɛɛl-/-bɛɛləx-   'fall ill/become cured'
Reciprocal: -ən-   e.g. -bɛl-/-bɛlən-   'hate/hate each other'

K. Additional Observations

Vocabulary Content

The vocabularies of these languages are closely related to those of B.60 and B.70, but they also contain a large proportion of peculiar items.

Sound Correspondences

The correspondences of 51 and 53 call for no comment, but in 52 there is the operation of umlaut, similar to what has been observed elsewhere in A.41 and A.42

only. This means that the seven radical vowels of the language do not correspond directly to the seven starred vowels, e.g.

*-u- -a → -ǫ-   e.g. *-gùmbá → ŋgǫǫmb   'porcupine'
*-u- -u → -ʉ-   e.g. *-dúŋgú → ndʉʉŋg   'pepper'

Internal Relationships

These are obscure since although B.51 is the least reduced, the reduction in B.52 and B.53 is in such different directions that it is difficult to compare them.

General Affinities

The languages of this group show clear relationships to B.40, B.60, and B.70, but little to the adjacent B.20 and B.30.

SOURCES

MS. notes on B.52 and B.53.
B.51: *Essai de Grammaire Douma*, by A. Reeb, 1895.
   Vocabulaire Aduma–Français and *Vocabulaire Français–Aduma*, by P. Dahin, 1895.

B.60 MBETE GROUP

B.61 *MBẸTẸ*
Spoken by about 15,000 people in Moyen Congo, to the north-east of Okondja.

B.62 *MBAMBA*, yi-
Spoken by about 12,000 people in Moyen Congo, to the north-east of Franceville.

B.63 *NDỤMBỌ*
Spoken by about 4,000 people in Moyen Congo, in the immediate neighbourhood of Franceville.

LINGUISTIC FEATURES

The type language is B.61 Mbẹtẹ.

A. Sound Patterns

Closed syllables and final syllabic nasals apparently do not occur in these languages.
There is a simple series of seven radical vowels with a distinction of quantity, e.g. 61: **-pas-** 'tear'; **-laas-** 'wear'.
The consonant sounds present few difficulties, although in 61 there are some rather unusual fricatives.
The tone patterns are difficult to describe in an outline, since they appear to vary according to the syntactical context. Examples of tone-slip, and even successive slips, will be found under the verbal conjugation.

B. Class System

The class systems of these languages are very similar and so the following outline from 61 may be considered as typical.

Independent Prefixes

Cl.	Prefix	Example	Gloss
Cl. 1/2	ọ-/a-	e.g. ọkásį/akásį	'woman/women'
Cl. 3/4	ọ-/ẹ-	e.g. ọsja/ẹsja	'rope/ropes'
Cl. 5/6	-/a-	e.g. yṉɔ́/ayṉɔ́	'spear/spears'
Cl. 7/4	kọ-/ẹ-	e.g. kọbɛlɛ/ẹbɛlɛ	'thigh/thighs'
Cl. 9/6	n-/an-	e.g. ntɔ́lọ/antɔ́lọ	'chest/chests'
Cl. 11/9	lẹ-/n-	e.g. lẹbáʃį/mbáʃį	'rib/ribs'

It will be noted that the same number is given to the class appearing as the plural of both Cl. 3 and Cl. 7. This is because there is no difference in the shape either of the independent or of the dependent prefixes. For the same reason there is only one class with an indeterminate nasal prefix, Cl. 9.

The following pair of words is peculiar in that the stem is different in the two classes, 61: Cl. 7/4 **kįįyį́/bįįbį́** 'thing/things'.

Dependent Prefixes

These are mainly similar in shape to the independent prefixes. The following list of words meaning 'this' will illustrate some other types of agreement.

Cl. 1. yụ Cl. 2. ba Cl. 3. yụ Cl. 4. bẹ
Cl. 5. yẹ Cl. 6. ma Cl. 9. yị Cl. 11. lẹ

An extra dependent prefix is attached with no linking element, e.g. 61: ẹbayá ẹ́n¹jɔ́ 'the roofs of the houses'.

D. NUMERALS

There is a simple decimal system of counting, '1'–'6' being dependent nominals and '7'–'9' independent. The shape of the stem of the numeral '2' is determined by the class in which the word occurs, e.g. 61: Cl. 4. dʒíɛ́lɛ́, Cl. 2. bvụ́ɔ́lɛ́, Cl. 6. mụ́ɔ́lɛ́.

E. NOMINAL SENTENCES

These do occur, although more frequently a copula is used, as in these examples from 61.

1. ọsịa yǔ ɔ́lẹ ŋɔ̆la   'this rope is long'
2. ẹsịa bě ɛ́lẹ ŋɔ̆la   'these ropes are long'

F. VERBAL SYSTEM

The following typical lists from 61 illustrate the fragmentary nature of the verbal systems.

Affirmative Conjugation

1. Past	-¹	-ẹ	e.g. lɛ́¹sụ́ɔ́mẹ	'we bought'
2. Future	-	-á	e.g. lɛ̂sụ́ɔ́má	'we shall buy'
3. Aspect of Completion	-¹mí¹-	-a	e.g. lɛ́¹mí¹sụ́ɔ́ma	'we have bought'
4. Aspect of Progress	-	-áŋá	e.g. lɛ̂sụ́ɔ́máŋá	'we are buying'

Negative Conjugation

1. Past	-¹kɔ́¹-	-a	e.g. lɛ́¹kɔ́¹sụ́ɔ́ma	'we did not buy'
2. Zero and Future	-kọ-	-a	e.g. lɛ̂kọsụ́ɔ́ma	'we do not buy'

Personal Prefixes

The following list refers to 61.

Cl. 1. 1st: n-   2nd: ọ-   3rd: a-
Cl. 2. 1st: lẹ- 2nd: lẹ- 3rd: a-

For the other classes the dependent verbal prefix is similar in shape to the independent prefix except in Cl. 9, where it is ẹ-. In 62 there is no prefix in the 2nd and 3rd persons of Cl. 1. There are no special object substitutes in these languages.

G. NOMINO-VERBALS

Nomino-Verbals are in Cl. 3, e.g. 61: ọsála 'working'.

H. EXTENSIONS

There are few regular extensions in these languages, but the following two occur in 61 in a number of cases:

    Reversive: -aɣ- e.g. -dựb-/-dựbaɣ- 'shut/open'
    Neuter: -jɣ- e.g. -nyựs-/-nyựsjɣ- 'awaken/awake'

K. ADDITIONAL OBSERVATIONS

Vocabulary Content

The vocabularies of these languages appear to occupy a position midway between those of B.20 and B.70.

Sound Correspondences

There are some characteristic correspondences with starred forms containing a nasal compound in position C_2, as in 61, e.g.:

    *-gòŋgá → yựɔ́ 'spear'
    *-kómb- → -kựɔ́m- 'sweep'
    *-cúmb- → -sựọ́m- 'buy'

General Affinities

The languages display a close relationship to B.50 and B.70, and a slight one to B.20. There does not appear to be much affinity between this group and the adjacent C.20.

SOURCES

MS. notes on B.61 and B.62.

B.70 TEKE GROUP

THESE languages are spoken by scattered groups mainly in the central area of Moyen Congo. Much of this plateau is waterless and so a large part of it is uninhabited.

B.71 *N. TEGE* and *NJINJDJ*
 B.71a *TEGE*, ka-
 Spoken in Moyen Congo in the neighbourhood of Eouo.
 B.71b *NJINJDJ*, ka-
 Spoken in Moyen Congo on both sides of the R. Alima in the region of Okoyo.

B.72 *MPŨ*, e̜- [Ngungulu]
 Spoken in Moyen Congo to the north of Gamboma.

B.73 *BOÕ* and *KU̜KẄA*
 B.73a *BOÕ*, e̜- [Boma]
 Spoken by a small group in Moyen Congo on the plateau inland from M'Pouya.
 B.73b *KU̜KẄA*
 Spoken in Moyen Congo by a small group on the plateau in the neighbourhood of Djambala.

B.74 *ḊEE*, esi-
 Spoken in Congo Belge, inland from the main river, to the north of the R. Kwa.

B.75 *TIO*, i- [Teke]
 Spoken by small groups in Moyen Congo and Congo Belge on both sides of Stanley Pool.

B.76 *WUMU*, i- [Wumbu, Mbunu]
 Spoken by a small group in Congo Belge, to the south of Léopoldville.

B.77 *S. W. TEGE*
 B.77a *TEGE*, i-
 Spoken in Moyen Congo in a narrow belt southwards from Zanaga.
 B.77b *LAALI*, i-
 Spoken by two groups of people in Moyen Congo, one to the east of Sibiti and the other to the north.
 B.77c *YAA*, i- [Yaka]
 Spoken in Moyen Congo by about 2,000 people in the region of Sibiti.

B.78 *FUMU*, i-
 This language is described in the work by Calloc'h, but at the present time no trace of the language can be found. It was presumably spoken to the north of Brazzaville by a small group now extinct.

B.70 TEKE GROUP·
LINGUISTIC FEATURES
The type language is B.71a Tɛgɛ.

A. SOUND PATTERNS

Closed syllables are rare in these languages. There is an unusual feature in 72 where both -w and -w̃ occur finally, e.g. ęláw 'fishhook', ęláw̃ 'tongue'. Occasionally there is a final syllabic nasal, as in 73b, e.g. -táán̄ '5'.

One characteristic of most of these languages, except 71 and 77, is the occurrence of stems and radicals consisting of a consonant followed by two vowels, e.g. 72: tų̀u 'animals', 73a: lębęi 'rib', 75: bio 'heap'.

The vowel series in radical position vary very greatly throughout the group. In 71 there is a series of seven radical vowels, with a distinction of quantity. In 72 there are so few radicals and stems with a consonant in second position that it is almost impracticable to refer to radical vowels. In 73–77 there is a series of five radical vowels with a distinction of quantity, which occurs in 77 even before a nasal compound. Nasalized vowels frequently occur in these languages, e.g. 72: dʒįį̃ 'tooth' (cf. dʒįį 'eye'), 75: -kuõ 'sweep' (cf. -kuo 'become enough').

The consonant sounds in first radical position sometimes include those with friction between the top teeth and the inside of the bottom teeth, e.g. 73: -ḳɔ̃ 'sweep', 75: -țío 'extract' (cf. -tío 'sell'). A semivowel with this articulation also occurs, e.g. 73b: w̧wa '9'. In 72 there are three different bilabial semivowels, e.g. -wa 'give' -w̧a 'pick up', -ẇa 'ascend', where the difference between -w- and -w̧- is simply that the latter has a much more tense tongue articulation. In 71 -kp- also occurs fairly frequently, although it is not clear where this is distinct from -kw-, e.g. kakpá 'yam'.

Tones are simple in 71–76 but more complicated in 77. Many lexical units are distinguished by tone, e.g. 71: -bę́l- 'dig', -bęl- 'carry'.

B. CLASS SYSTEM

The class systems throughout the group vary in details only. The following outline refers to 71.

Cl. 1/2	ǫ-/a-	e.g. ǫkálį/akálį	'woman/women'
Cl. 3/4	ǫ-/ę-	e.g. ǫsįrá/esįrá	'tendon/tendons'
Cl. 5/6	-/a-	e.g. sála/asála	'work/jobs'
Cl. 7/4	ka-/ę-	e.g. kalɔ́yɔ/elɔ́yɔ	'thing/things'
Cl. 9/6	n-/an-	e.g. mbįelį/ambįelį	'knife/knives'
Cl. 11/9	la-/n-	e.g. lasálá/ntʃálá	'feather/feathers'

In vowel junction:

Cl. 5/4	dʒį-/mbį-	e.g. dʒįįrį/mbįįrį	'eye/eyes'
Cl. 7/8	kų-/ndʒų-	e.g. kųɔyɔ/ndʒųɔyɔ	'arm/arms'

The other languages of the group have Cl. 7 i- (or ę-) and Cl. 11 li- (or lę-). Zero prefix in Cl. 5 is a feature of the whole group, but there is a regular Cl. 8 prefix bi- (or bį-) in 73–77. The occurrence of the words 'eye/eyes' in Cl. 5/4 is typical of all of these languages. There is m- in the prefix of Cl. 1, 3, 4, and 6 in 74, 76, and 77.

B.70 TEKE GROUP

Dependent Prefixes

There are few series of dependent prefixes; in most cases they are identical in shape with the independent prefixes, except that the agreement for Cl. 5 is the same as that for Cl. 11. In 74–77 some stems require double dependent prefixes, as in 77c, e.g. Cl. 3/4 **wumunene/miminene** 'big'.

An extra dependent prefix is attached with no linking vowel, e.g. 73a: **bį ękyǫ įmfũ** 'these are the cloths of the chief'.

C. Possessives

There are no special possessive stems in these languages, instead personal substitutes are used with a dependent prefix, as in 75, e.g. **biko bime (binde)** 'my (his) cloths'.

D. Numerals

There is a simple decimal system of counting throughout the group, '1'–'6' being dependent nominals and '7'–'9' independent. The stem of the numeral '2' in most of these languages is peculiar in that it is -ɔlɛ (or -ole) in Cl. 2, 4, and 6, but -ɛlɛ (or ele) in the others, e.g. 71: Cl. 6 **myɔlɛ**, Cl. 8 **dʒɛlɛ**. The chief exceptions to this are 72: **-aa** and 77: **-ole**.

E. Nominal Sentences

These regularly occur except in 71. The following typical examples are from 77a

1. **íko ki kiɣivê** 'this cloth is good'
2. **bíko bi bibivê** 'these cloths are good'

F. Verbal System

Conjugation

The tense signs in these languages are few in number. Frequently there are two one-word tenses only, as in 71a, e.g.:

1. Past **-į** e.g. **leparį** 'we tore'
2. Zero and Future **-a** e.g. **lĕpara** 'we tear'

Negation

There are usually no negative tenses as such. Negative sentences are formed in one of two ways.

(1) A special auxiliary negative radical may be used, the main radical then being in the form of a nomino-verbal. In this case there is usually a negative element at the end of the sentence, while a nominal object will precede the nomino-verbal, as in 71a, e.g.:

1. **lekɛ́ kakɔ ǫpara ŋį** 'we did not tear the cloth'
2. **lĕká kakɔ ǫpara ŋį** 'we do not tear the cloth'

(2) There may be a negative element prefixed to the verbal with another at the end of the sentence, as in 75, e.g.:

bé libúlí mbío 'you have smashed the pot'
bé kalibúlí mbío wo 'you have not smashed the pot'

Personal Prefixes

The following typical list refers to 71*a*.

Cl. 1. 1st: **n-** 2nd: - 3rd: -
Cl. 2. 1st: **lẹ-** 2nd: **lẹ-** 3rd: **a-**

The peculiarity of this language, in common with most of the others in this group, is that there is no prefix for the 2nd and 3rd persons of Cl. 1. There are no distinct object substitutes.

G. Nomino-Verbals

These have a prefix **ọ-**, **o-**, or **u-**, which has its own agreements and should probably be numbered Cl. 15, e.g. 75: **otío** 'to sell'.

H. Extensions

Extended radicals occur, but their relationship to simple radicals is obscure and no clear rules can be formulated. The following example from 71*a* will illustrate the kind of thing that occurs, e.g. **-dʒṳm-/-dʒṳbṳ-** 'become extinguished/extinguish'.

K. Additional Observations

Vocabulary Content

There is a large proportion of the vocabularies of these languages peculiar to the group, and there are very few items common to the group and Bantu languages elsewhere that are not also common to adjacent groups.

Sound Correspondences

These are frequently complicated and difficult to illustrate in detail. The feature most characteristic of these languages is the correspondence for *ŋg in second radical position as in 71, e.g. *-**gàŋgà** → **ọŋgaa** 'medicine man', *-**gòŋgò** → **ọŋgṳọ** 'back'.

Internal Relationships

The most complex features occur in 71 on the one hand and 77 on the other. The greatest reduction is in 72 and 73.

General Affinities

These languages show a close relationship with A.50, A.60, and A.80, but only slight affinities with C.20 and C.30 to the north and east, and with H.10 to the south.

SOURCES

MS. notes for the whole group.
B.75: *A Vocabulary of the Kiteke*, by A. Sims, 1888.
B.78: *Vocabulaire Français–Ifumu (Bateke)*, by J. Calloc'h, 1911.

B.80 TENDE-YANZI GROUP

B.81 *TJINI*, ki- [Tende]
Spoken in Congo Belge inland from the main river from Bolobo.

B.82 *BOMA*, i-
Spoken in Congo Belge by about 8,000 people inland from Mushie on the north bank of the R. Fimi and the R. Kwa and also on the opposite bank of the R. Kwa.

B.83 *MFINU*, e- [Mfunika, Mfununga]
Spoken in Congo Belge by about 20,000 people in the plateau to the north-east of Léopoldville.

B.84 *DJIA* and *SAKATA*
  B.84a *DJIA*, ki-
  Spoken in Congo Belge to the north of the R. Fimi to the west of L. Léopold II.
  B.84b *SAKATA*, ki- [Lesa, Tete]
  Spoken in Congo Belge between the R. Lukenie and the R. Kasai, west of the 19th meridian east.

B.85 *YANS*, i̧- [Yanzi]
Spoken in Congo Belge to the south of the R. Kasai near its confluence with the R. Kamtsha to below Banningville.

B.86 *ŊGUL*, i̧- [Ngoli]
Spoken in Congo Belge to the south of the R. Kasai near its confluence with the R. Kamtsha.

B.87 *DĮ*, i- and *DZĮD*, i̧-
Spoken in Congo Belge mainly between the R. Kasai and R. Kwilu, north of Idiofa.

B.88 *MBUUN*, i̧- [Mbunda]
Spoken in Congo Belge to the east of the R. Kwilu in the region of Kikwit and as far east as the R. Longe.

LINGUISTIC FEATURES

A. SOUND PATTERNS

Closed syllables are rare in 81–84, but common in 85–88, e.g. 85: **pap** 'wing', **sok** 'axe'. In these and similar cases a final stop is not normally released.

The vowel series of these languages vary very greatly. In 81 and 82 there is a simple series of seven radical vowels, with a distinction of quantity in 81 only, but there is not very much difference in the tongue position for the open and close **i** and **u** in these languages. In 83 where monosyllabic are commoner than dissyllabic stems and radicals there are quite different series of vowels in the two cases, both being very involved from the point of view both of quality and of quantity. The vowel series of 84 and 85 are so complicated that they cannot be described simply. In both languages centralized vowels of many kinds are very common, e.g. 84*b* mpöi 'knife', jbuj 'breast', mpëj 'water'. There are many nasalized vowels in 85, e.g. ãdĩĩ 'oranges', mjdĩĩ 'pots'.

The consonants of the languages of this group display a number of peculiarities. In 81 there is an unusual syllable wu̯-, e.g. -wu̯ol- 'open'. In 82 uvular fricatives are common, this being the usual articulation of the sound spelt x in xoxo 'arm'. In 83 palatal affricates occur, e.g. -cçɔ 'chase', -jzǫ 'paddle'. There is a distinction between l and ḷ in final position in 84, the second of these two sounds having a dental articulation, e.g. mábul 'villages', makuḷ 'gourds'.

The tone-patterns of these languages are almost as involved as their vowels, and in most cases it is impossible to quote the tones of a word in abstraction. Examples of tone-slip in 85 may be seen under the section on Nominal Sentences.

B. Class System

There is some variation in the class systems of these languages, so the following outline from 81 will serve to give a general impression only.

Independent Prefixes

	Cl. 1/2	mu-/ba-	e.g. mukáati/bakáati	'wife/wives'
	Cl. 3/4	mu-/mj-	e.g. mukolo/mjkolo	'heart/hearts'
	Cl. 5/6	i-/ma-	e.g. isaá/masaá	'roof/roofs'
	Cl. 7/8	ki-/bi-	e.g. kikjjni/bikjjni	'load/loads'
	Cl. 9/10	n-/n-	e.g. ŋguone/ŋguone	'garden/gardens'
	Cl. 11/10	li-/n-	e.g. líkwá/ŋkwá	'bone/bones'
	Cl. 14	bu-	e.g. bukutj	'shame'

In vowel junction:

	Cl. 3/4	mu-/mj-	e.g. muomo/mjeme	'fetish/fetishes'
	Cl. 5/4	dj-/mj-	e.g. djjnj/mjjnj	'tooth/teeth'
	Cl. 14/6	wa-/ma-	e.g. waáti/maáti	'canoe/canoes'
	Cl. 15/4	ku-/mj-	e.g. kuulu/mjili	'leg/legs'

Among the last four pairs are two examples of the peculiar behaviour of some stems in this language, it being impossible to assign a definite quality to the vowels in such cases.

The principal points of difference in the other languages are the following. In 83–88 Cl. 7 is e- or j-, while in all the rest of the group except 82 and 84 Cl. 10 is used as a plural of Cl. 11 only, the plural corresponding to Cl. 9 being in Cl. 6.

Dependent Prefixes

In 81–84 these are mainly similar to the independent except in Cl. 9/10 where there is 81: i-/a-, 82: e-/j-, 83: i-/i-, 84: nj-/zj-. In 83 and 85 there are double dependent prefixes in some cases, e.g. 85: Cl. 3/4 w̌wonɛnónɛn/ mjjnɛnjnɛn 'big'.

An extra dependent prefix is attached with no linking vowel, e.g. 84*b*: beʃə́ bemwé 'clothes of the child'.

D. NUMERALS

In most cases the numerals '1'–'6' are dependent nominals and '7'–'9' independent. Higher numerals are usually based on a decimal system of counting, but the multiples of ten often display some peculiarities. In 83 the Cl. 6 word **maku** 'tens' is used for from '20' to '60', but for '70' and '80' there are **lekuncǫaamo** and **lekumpuomo** while '90' is **eowa**.

In 82 there is a special word **mwabi** '20', while '30'–'60' have the stem of the multiplier with the independent prefix of Cl. 3, e.g. **mutaanu** '50', but '70' is in Cl. 4 and '80' in Cl. 11, **mǐʃamu** '70', **linaana** '80'. In 84*b* '30'–'90' are in Cl. 3, but '20' is simply the plural word corresponding to '10', **dʒõ** '10', **m̥aõ** '20'.

E. NOMINAL SENTENCES

These occur in some of these languages, but others, such as 81–83, normally use a copula of some kind. The following examples are from 85.

1. **kye llá lę́'lębę** 'this egg is bad'
2. **makye mmá má'mábę** 'these eggs are bad'

F. VERBAL SYSTEM

There is not much in common between the verbal systems of some of these languages, so it is of scarcely any value to give a typical conjugation. Instead two samples of the affirmative tenses will be given.

Affirmative Conjugation

In 81 there are the following tenses.

1. Past   -įʃ   e.g. **litįmįʃ**   'we dug'
2. Future and Aspect of Progress   -a   e.g. **litįmá**   'we shall dig'
3. Aspect of Completion   -į   e.g. **lítįmį**   'we have dug'
4. Aspect of Repetition   -aa   e.g. **lítįmaa**   'we usually dig'

In 85 the following are some of the tenses that occur.

1. Past   -ti-   e.g. **bí atí'fúr**   'we paid'
2. Future   -aya-   e.g. **bí kiayafur**   'we shall pay'
3. Aspect of Completion -ã-   e.g. **bí kyãfur**   'we have paid'
4. Aspect of Repetition -a- -a- e.g. **bí kyafúrafúr**   'we pay'

The tenses in 83 are mainly distinguished by the use of different tone-patterns, but there is also a longer base in which the first syllable of the radical is reduplicated, e.g.:

lefúrú   'we shall pay'
lefufuru 'we usually pay'
lefufúrú 'we shall regularly pay'

Negation

In most of these languages there are no negative tenses, instead special negative elements are used before the verbal and at the end of the sentence, as in 81, e.g.:

kalítįmįʃ kɔ 'we did not give'

Personal Prefixes

These vary greatly throughout the group. There is usually **n-** for the 1st person of Cl. 1 and **ba-** for the 3rd person of Cl. 2, otherwise 81–84 have **u-** for the 2nd person of Cl. 1 and **a-** for the 3rd. In 84a however, as in 85, there are different prefixes for the same person in different tenses. The 2nd person of Cl. 2 is **bu-** in 81 and 82, **le-** in 83, **ne-** in 84, and **la-** in 85. In most of these languages a personal substitute has also to be used in every case.

G. NOMINO-VERBALS

These usually have a prefix **u-** (*or* **o-**) which has its own agreements, e.g. 83: **odịrịị** 'to think', 85: **úyịb** 'to steal'.

H. EXTENSIONS

A characteristic of this whole group is the absence of regular types of extended radical. In 81 there is a most unusual feature, some extensions occurring between the two radical consonants, e.g.:

Applied:	-ne-	e.g. -tịm-/-tịnem-	'dig/dig for'
	-(v)-	e.g. -sal-/-saal-	'work/work for'
		-son-/-soon-	'write/write for'
Causative:	-se-	e.g. -bịk-/-bịsek-	'become cured/cure'

K. ADDITIONAL OBSERVATIONS

Vocabulary Content

There are many peculiar items in the vocabularies of these languages. Besides those which show a relationship to Bantu languages outside the area, there are a few which are apparently similar to items found in languages of Zone A.

Sound Correspondences

These are so complex for the majority of these languages, that it is not possible even to illustrate the more interesting ones without going right outside the scope of this work.

Internal Relationships

The most complex languages are 81 and 82, while the degree of reduction in the others is fairly uniform, although such reduction is by no means of the same kind in each case.

General Affinities

The affinities of these languages are almost entirely in the direction of the other groups of Zone B. There is very little close relationship with the adjacent languages of Groups C.30, C.60, and C.80; L.10 and H.10 and H.30.

SOURCES

MS. notes on B.81–85.
B.87: *Grammaire de l'Idzing de la Kamtsha*, by J. Mertens and V. van Bulck, 1938.
B.87: *Dictionnaire Idzing–Français, Français–Idzing*, J. Mertens, 1939.

C.10 NGUNDI GROUP

C.11 ŊGǪNDĮ [Ngundi]
Spoken by a small group of people in fishing villages along the R. Sanga between Nola and Bayanga in Oubangui-Chari.

C.12 PANDĘ and BǪGƆŊGƆ

C.12a PANDĘ [Linzeli]
Spoken by a number of isolated groups of people in Oubangui-Chari and Moyen Congo. The most westerly group is along the shores of the R. Mambéré above Nola. The others are scattered throughout the forest for about 100 miles to the east of the river.

C.12b BǪGƆŊGƆ [Bukongo]
Spoken in Oubangui-Chari just inland from the east bank of the R. Mambéré, parallel to the first area given for 12a.

C.13 MBATĮ
Spoken along the R. Lobaye to the south-west of M'Baiki in Oubangui-Chari.

C.14 MBǪMǪTABA [Bamitaba]
Spoken in Moyen Congo in isolated groups in the swampy forest between the R. Sanga and the R. Oubangui, to the north-east of Ikelemba.

C.15 BǪŊGĮLĮ [Bungiri]
Spoken in Moyen Congo to the west of the R. Sanga downstream from Ouesso and Ikélemba.

LINGUISTIC FEATURES

The type language is C.11 Ŋgǫndį.

A. Sound Patterns

Closed syllables and final syllabic nasals apparently do not occur.

There is a simple series of seven radical vowels throughout the group with no distinction of quantity.

The voiced stops are imploded in most of these languages, while in 11 there is a common use of the fricatives, ð, θ, f, φ, and v.

The tones are simple throughout the group, but tone-slip occurs in 12b.

B. Class System

The following outline refers to 11, and apart from details is typical of the other languages except 12.

Independent Prefixes

Cl. 1/2	mọ-/ba-	e.g. mọtọ/batọ	'person/persons'
Cl. 3/4	mọ-/mẹ-	e.g. mọkɔŋgɔ/mẹkɔŋgɔ	'back/backs'
Cl. 5/6	į-/ma-	e.g. įbɔ́ŋgɔ́/mabɔ́ŋgɔ́	'knee/knees'
Cl. 7/8	ẹ-/bį-	e.g. ẹbẹθẹ́/bįbẹθẹ́	'bone/bones'
Cl. 9/6	n-/man-	e.g. mbɔ́ka/mambɔ́ka	'garden/gardens'
Cl. 14/6	bọ-/ma-	e.g. bọka/maka	'mat/mats'

With special stems:
There are words of the following kind in 11, in which it is not clear which is the stem and which the prefix.

    Cl. 3/4 e.g. **mɔ́ŋgɔ/mɛ́ŋgɔ** 'corpse/corpses'
    Cl. 7/8 e.g. **yɔ́mbɔ/bɛ́mbɔ** 'broom/brooms'

The two dialects 12a and 12b are sub-Bantu, and have a fragmentary class system, in which **ba-** is normally prefixed to all plural words.

Dependent Prefixes

These are similar in shape to the independent prefixes in most cases except in Cl. 9 and Cl. 10 where we find **ẹ-/į-**.

An extra dependent prefix is attached with **-a-**, e.g. 11: **mįkụlẹ mįamamɔ́lį** 'horns of the goats'.

D. NUMERALS

In 11 and 12 the numerals '1'–'9' are dependent nominals, '6'–'9' being of the pattern '5' plus '1', while score counting is used from '20' to '90'. In the other languages there is a simple decimal system of counting, '1'–'5' being dependent nominals and '6'–'9' independent.

E. NOMINAL SENTENCES

These regularly occur, except in 12, the following example from 15 being typical.

1. **mọndį́kį mɔ́ mọsánda**   'this rope is long'
2. **mįndį́kį mį́ mįsánda**   'these ropes are long'

F. VERBAL SYSTEM

The following typical outline refers to 11.

Affirmative Conjugation

1. Past   -   -į   e.g. **tọθɔ́mbį**   'we bought'
2. Future   -kọ- -á   e.g. **tọkọθɔ́mbá**   'we shall buy'
3. Aspect of Progress   -ɸɔ́- -a   e.g. **tọɸɔ́θɔ́mba**   'we are buying'

Negative Conjugation

1. Past   -ta- -į   e.g. **tọtaθɔ́mbį**   'we did not buy'
2. Future   -į- -a   e.g. **tọįθɔ́mba**   'we shall not buy'

In 12b there are two negative elements **tẹ** and **wa** which occur before the verbal and in final position respectively.

Personal Prefixes
The following list refers to 11.
Cl. 1. 1st: **na-**   2nd: **ǫ-**   3rd: **a-**
Cl. 2. 1st: **tǫ-**   2nd: **nǫ-**   3rd: **ba-**
In 12*b* there is **lę-** and in 15 **bǫ-** for both the 1st and 2nd persons of Cl. 2.

G. Nomino-Verbals
These are in Cl. 5, e.g. 15: **iʃɔ́mba** 'to buy'.

H. Extensions
Apart from 12, these languages have many extended radicals, the following examples being typical.

11: Causative:	-ęŏ-	e.g. -θɔ́mb-/-θɔ́mbęŏ-	'buy/sell'
15: Causative:	-iz-	e.g. -ʃíl-/-ʃílįz-	'become finished/finish'
Passive:	-ib-	e.g. -ɸúnd-/-ɸúndib-	'accuse/be accused'

K. Additional Observations
Vocabulary Content
There is a high proportion of the vocabularies of these languages that is also common to the adjacent Group C.30.

Sound Correspondences
The following are one or two of the interesting correspondences found in 11.

*nj → ŏ	e.g. *-jògù̀ → ŏɔkụ	'elephant'
*d → zero	e.g. *-gíd- → -ké̜-	'do'
*t → l	e.g. *-túnd- → -lɔ́nd-	'become full'

Internal Relationships
The most reduced member of the group is the sub-Bantu cluster C.12. The most complex member is C.15 which displays most of the characteristics of a full Zone C language.

General Affinities
Apart from some common loan-words from the nearby non-Bantu languages, as **bɔɸɛ** '10', **gɔmai** '100' in C.11, these languages are related more closely to C.30 than to C.20. They show little if any immediate affinities to the nearby groups to the west, A.80 and A.90.

SOURCES
MS. notes on the whole group except C.*12a* and C.13.
C.11 and C.*12a*: 'Notes sur les Langues des Pygmées de la Sanga', by Dr. Ouzilleau, in *Revue d'Ethnographie et de Sociologie*, Paris, 1911.

C.20 MBOSHI GROUP

C.21 *MBOKO*
Spoken in Moyen Congo in the region of Odzala.

C.22 *AKWA*
Spoken in Moyen Congo in the region of Makoua.

C.23 *ŊGARE*
Spoken in Moyen Congo to the west of Makoua.

C.24 *KOYO*
Spoken in Moyen Congo in the region of Fort Rousset.

C.25 *MBƆSI* [Mboshi]
Spoken in Moyen Congo on both sides of the R. Alima to the south of Fort Rousset.

C.26 *KWALA*, li̯-
Spoken in Moyen Congo mainly to the west of the lower reaches of the R. Likouala.

C.27 *KỤBA*, li̯-
Spoken in Moyen Congo on both sides of the lower reaches of the R. Alima.

LINGUISTIC FEATURES

The type language is C.22 Akwa.

A. Sound Patterns

There are no closed syllables or final syllabic nasals in this group.

There is a simple series of seven radical vowels with no distinction of quantity. Sometimes two identical vowels occur in juxtaposition, but the second can be treated as a different syllable, e.g. 22: **báá** 'they'.

The voiced stops are normally exploded. One peculiarity of the consonant sounds is that long consonants may occur at the beginning of syllables, e.g. 22: **jvva** '9', **bba** 'river'. The distinctions **t/d** and **k/g** apparently do not occur intervocalically in this group; in position C_1 the nasalized stop occurs while in C_2 its voiced counterpart.

The tone patterns present few difficulties, tone-slip apparently does not occur.

B. Class System

The following typical outline refers to 22.

Independent Prefixes

The peculiarity of the prefixes is that they mainly consist of single vowels. This results in a similarity of shape in Classes 1, 3, 11, and 14, while the plural to Classes 1,

5, 9, and 14 is not only identical in shape, but also in agreements and must therefore be regarded as a single class, e.g.:

Cl. 1/2	ọ-/a-	e.g. ọbụrụ/abụrụ	'stranger/strangers'
Cl. 3/4	ọ-/ị-	e.g. ọtẹ́ma/ịtẹ́ma	'heart/hearts'
Cl. 5/2	ị-/a-	e.g. ịkɔŋgɔ́/akɔŋgɔ́	'spear/spears'
Cl. 7/4	ẹ-/ị-	e.g. ẹbɔ́gɔ/ịbɔ́gɔ	'arm/arms'
Cl. 9/2	n̪-/an̪-	e.g. ŋgálá/aŋgálá	'back/backs'
Cl. 11/9	ọ-/n̪-	e.g. ọbandʒẹ́/mbandʒẹ́	'rib/ribs'
Cl. 14/2	ọ-/a-	e.g. ọlọ́mbọ/alọ́mbọ	'dance/dances'

In vowel junction:

Cl. 1/2	m̥w-/b-	e.g. m̥wána/bána	'child/children'
Cl. 3/4	m̥w-/mị-	e.g. m̥wánọ/mịánọ	'mouth/mouths'
Cl. 5/4	d-/m-	e.g. dịna/mịna	'tooth/teeth'
Cl. 14/2	v-/m-	e.g. vátọ/mátọ	'canoe/canoes'

With one-syllable stems:

| Cl. 3/4 | m-/mị- | e.g. mtọ/mịtọ́ | 'head/heads' |

With special stems:

In words of the following kind from 22, it is not clear which is the stem and which the prefix, e.g.:

    Cl. 3/4 mɔnya/mɛnya 'fire/fires'

Dependent Prefixes

In 22 these are almost identical with the following words meaning 'this': 1. wọ 2. ba 3. wọ 4. bị 5. dị 7. yẹ 9. yẹ 11. lọ 14. bọ.

An extra dependent prefix is linked with -a-, e.g. 22: ẹbagá yandágọ 'wall of the house'. When the nominal bearing such a prefix refers to a person then the linking element is -ámbâ-, e.g. 22: ẹsẹ́gẹ yámbâmwána 'hoe of the child'.

D. NUMERALS

The numerals '1'–'5' are dependent nominals, '6'–'9' being independent. The relationship of the multiples of 10 to the numerals '1'–'9' is sufficiently peculiar to be noted. The following typical words from 22 fall into four main types:

nyộmbaa/-baa '20/2', nyộtọ́bá/ọtọ́bá '60/6', nyộmwambẹ/mwambẹ '80/8' nyị́tʃádọ/-sádọ '40/4'

akọ́manị/-nị '40/4', akwátanọ/-tanọ '50/5', akwẹ́tʃambọ/tʃambọ '70/7' tɔvva/ịvva '90/9'

E. NOMINAL SENTENCES

These do not normally occur, sentences of the following kind from 22 with a copula being typical.

    1. ọpáná' wọ́ wódí wɔ́ɔnɛ 'this tree is big'
    2. ịpáná' bị bịdí bịịnênɛ 'these trees are big'

A peculiarity that occurs in several of these languages is also illustrated in these sentences, the stem of the dependent nominal being doubled in a plural sentence.

F. Verbal System

Conjugation

There are very few tenses in these languages, the following example from 22 where there are two simple tenses is typical.

 1. Past   -į   e.g. ŋgá nįsómbį   'I bought'
 2. Zero and Future   -a   e.g. ŋgá nįsǫ́mba   'I buy'

Negation

Negative tenses are even fewer in number than the affirmative. In 22 there is one true negative tense only, which serves as the negative corresponding to Tense 1, e.g.:

    ŋgá nįlǫ̌sǫ́mba ka   'I did not buy'

In all other cases in 22 an invariable word is used consisting of the radical with the affixes ǫ- -a, e.g.:

    ŋgá ǫsǫ́mba ka   'I do not buy'

Negative sentences in each of these languages end with some negative element such as **ka** in the above examples.

Personal Prefixes

The personal prefixes are always preceded by personal substitutes which are therefore quoted with the prefixes in this typical list from 22.

   Cl. 1. 1st: **ŋgá nį-**   2nd: **nɔ́ ǫ-**   3rd: **nɛ́ na-**
   Cl. 2. 1st: **bįsǫ́ lǫ́-**   2nd: **bįnǫ́ lǫ́-**   3rd: **bâá bá-**

There are no distinct object substitutes in these languages.

Relative Construction

The verbal always agrees with the antecedent, e.g.:

   bá bádį akɔŋgɔ́ bábų́nyį   'they are the spears that broke'

With an object antecedent the nominal referring to the logical subject follows the verbal, e.g.:

   yę́ įdį fwá įsǫ́mbį ǫyįęų   'this is the cloth the woman bought'
   bá bádį afwá básǫ́mbį ǫyįęų   'they are the cloths the woman bought'

G. Nomino-Verbals

These are in Cl. 5, e.g. 22: **įsǫ́mba** 'buying'.

H. Extensions

Radicals with extensions do occur, but regular patterns appear to be rare.

K. Additional Observations

Vocabulary Content

Apart from the nucleus of items common to most Bantu languages, the vocabularies of this group appear to contain many peculiar items.

C.20 MBOSHI GROUP

Sound Correspondences

There is not much of interest in the sound correspondences of this group of languages, apart from the following typical ones from 22.

$*d_1 \to l$	e.g.	*-dóbò → ilóbɔ	'fishhook'
$*d_2 \to$ zero	e.g.	*-túdù → tǫ̂	'chest'
$*g_1 \to k$	e.g.	*-gı̣dá → akjá	'blood'
$*g_2 \to \dot{g}$	e.g.	*-búgà → mbǫ́ġa	'village'

Internal Relationships

There is little apparent difference in the complexity of the members of the group.

General Affinities

Although of the same general type as many of the other groups of Zone C, this group is very much one on its own. It contains scarcely any typical Bantu features not also found in adjacent languages.

SOURCES

MS. notes on the whole group except C.21 and C.23.

INDEX OF LANGUAGES

Abo. *See* Baŋkɔn
Adjumba. *See* Dyumba
Akpwakum. *See* Kwakum
Akwa (C.22), 88
Apindji. *See* Tsɔgɔ

Baakpɛ (A.22), 20
Bacɛŋga (A.64), 36
Badjia. *See* Bakja
Bafia Group, 33
Bafia. *See* Kpa
Bafɔ (A.15a), 15
Bakaka. *See* Kaa
Bakja (A.72c), 40
Bakɔgɔ (A.43b), 28
Bakum. *See* Kwakum
Bakundu (A.11c), 15
Bakwele. *See* Bɛkwil
Bakwiri. *See* Baakpɛ
Balom. *See* Fa'
Balɔŋ (A.13), 15
Balundu. *See* Lundu
Bamitaba. *See* Mbɔmɔtaba
Bamvele. *See* Bëbëlë
Bane. *See* Bënë
Banend. *See* Banɛn
Banɛn (A.44), 28
Bangomo. *See* Kɛlɛ or Ŋgɔm
Banɔɔ (A.32a), 24
Baŋkɔn (A.42), 28
Bapɔkɔ (A. 32b), 24
Baruɛ (A.12), 15
Basa Group, 28
Basa. *See* Mbɛnɛ
Basosi. *See* Swasɔ
Batanga (A.32), 24
Batanga (A.11d), 15
Bati (A.65), 36
Bëbëlë (A.73a), 40
Bënë (A.74b), 40
Bɛŋga (A.34), 24
Betsinga. *See* Bacɛŋga
Bɛkwil (A.85b), 45
Bima (A.11d), 15
Bimbia. *See* Su
Bobili. *See* Gbïgbïl
Bɔgɔŋgɔ (C.12b), 85
Boma. *See* Boõ
Boma (B.82), 81
Bombo. *See* Mpõmpõ
Bɔmbɔkɔ (A.21), 20
Bɔmwali (A.87), 46
Bɔŋgili (C.15), 85
Boõ (B.73a), 77
Bɔŋkɛn (A.14), 15
Bubɛ (A.31), 24
Bube-Benga Group, 24

Bubi (B.22c), 59
Bukongo. *See* Bɔgɔŋgɔ
Bulu. *See* Sɛkiyani
Bulu (A.74a), 40
Bungiri. *See* Bɔŋgili

Di (B.87), 81
Djanti. *See* Ŋgayaba
Djem. *See* Njëm
Djia (B.84a), 81
Duala Group, 20
Duala (A.24), 20
Duma (B.51), 70
Dyumba (B.11d), 55
Dzimu. *See* Njëm
Dziŋ (B.87), 81

Ediya. *See* Bubɛ
Ekumbɛ (A.11e), 15
Elong. *See* Löŋ
Etɔn (A.71), 40
Ewodi. *See* Ɔli
Ewɔndɔ (A.72a), 40

Fa' (A.51), 33
Fak. *See* Fa'
Faŋ (A.75), 41
Fumu (B.78), 77

Galwa (B.11c), 55
Gbïgbïl (A.73b), 40

Isubu. *See* Su

Kaa (A.15f), 15
Kaalɔŋ (A.52), 33
Kaka Group, 50
Kaka. *See* Kakɔ
Kakɔ (A.93), 50
Kande (B.32), 64
Kele Group, 59
Kɛlɛ (B. 22a), 59
Koko. *See* Mbɛnɛ
Koko. *See* Bakɔgɔ
Kombe (A.33), 24
Kɔnabɛm (A.85a), 45
Konabembe. *See* Kɔnabɛm
Kɔta (B.25), 59
Kɔyɔ (C.24), 88
Kozime. *See* Njëm
Kɔɔsɔ (A.15b), 15
Kpa (A.53), 33
Kuba (C.27), 88
Kukwa (B.73b), 77
Kundu, W. *See* Baruɛ
Kwakum (A.91), 50
Kwala (C.26), 88

Laali (B.77b), 77
Lemande. *See* Mandi
Lesa. *See* Sakata
Linzeli. *See* Pandɛ
Lɔmbi (A.41), 28
Löŋ (A.15d), 15
Lue. *See* Baruɛ
Lumbu (B.44), 67
Lundu (A.11a), 15
Lundu-Mbo Group, 15

Mahongwe. *See* Kɔta
Maka-Njem Group, 45
Makaa (A.83), 45
Make. *See* Faŋ
Malimba. *See* Mulimba
Mandi (A.46), 28
Maŋgisa (A.63), 36
Mbamba (B.62), 74
Mbaŋwe (B.23), 59
Mbati (C.13), 85
Mbete Group, 74
Mbɛtɛ (B.61), 74
Mbɛnɛ (A.43a), 28
Mbimu. *See* Mpjɛmɔ
Mbo (A.15), 15
Mboko. *See* Bɔmbɔkɔ
Mbɔkɔ (C.21), 88
Mbɔmɔtaba (C.14), 85
Mboshi Group, 88
Mboshi. *See* Mbɔsi
Mbɔ (A.15g), 15
Mbɔŋ (A.52), 33
Mbɔŋgɛ (A.11e), 15
Mbɔsi (C.25), 88
Mbunda. *See* Mbuun
Mbunu. *See* Wumu
Mbuun (B.88), 81
Mɛdjimɛ (A.86a), 45
Mfinu (B.83), 81
Mfunika. *See* Mfinu
Mfununga. *See* Mfinu
Mitsogo. *See* Tsɔgɔ
Mpjɛmɔ (A. 86c), 45
Mpɔŋgwɛ (B.11a), 55
Mpõmpõ (A.86b), 45
Mpũ (B.72), 77
Mulimba (A.27), 20
Muŋgɔ (A.26), 20
Mvele. *See* Mbɛnɛ
Mvëlë (A.72b), 40
Mvumbo (A.81), 45
Myene Cluster, 55

Naka. *See* Bapɔkɔ
Ndumbɔ (B.63), 74
Nenũ (A.15e), 15

INDEX OF LANGUAGES

Ngoli. See Ŋgul
Ngolo. See Ŋgɔrɔ
Ngumba. See Mvumbo
Ngundi. See Ŋgɔndi
Ngundi Group, 85
Ngungulu. See Mpũ
Njabi. See Nzɛbi
Njabi Group, 70
Njëm (A.84), 45
Njininį (B.71b), 77
Nkosi. See Kɔɔsə
Noho. See Banɔɔ
Noko. See Banɔɔ
Ntum. See Faŋ
Nyokon. See Nyɔ̃'ɔ
Nyɔ̃'ɔ (A.45), 28
Nzɛbi (B.52), 70
Ɖee (B.74), 77
Ŋgarɛ, (C.23), 88
Ŋgayaba (A.54), 33
Ŋgɔndi (C.11), 85
Ŋgɔrɔ (A.11b), 15
Ŋgom (B.22b), 59
Ŋgɔrɔ (A.61), 36
Ŋgul (B.86), 81
Ŋkɔmi (B.11e), 55

Okande (B.32), 64

Ɔli (A.25), 20
Orungu. See Rɔŋgo

Pakum. See Kwakum
Pandɛ (C.12a), 85
Pangwe. See Faŋ
Pɔl (A.92a), 50
Pɔŋgɔ (A.26), 20
Pomɔ (A.92b), 50
Puku. See Bapɔkɔ
Punu (B.43), 67

Rombi. See Lɔmbi
Rɔŋgo (B.11b), 55

Sakata (B.84b), 81
Sanaga Group, 36
Saŋgu (B.42), 67
Sɛkiyani (B.21), 59
Shake. See Kɔta
Shango. See Saŋgu
Sheke. See Sɛkiyani
Shira. See Sira
Shira-Punu Group, 67
Sira (B.41), 67
So (A.82), 45
Su (A.23), 20
Swasɔ (A.15c), 15

Tege (B.77a), 77
Teke Group, 77
Teke. See Tio
Tende. See Tiini
Tende-Yanzi Group, 81
Tete. See Sakata
Tege (B.71a), 77
Tiini (B.81), 81
Tio (B.75), 77
Tsaaŋgi (B.53), 70
Tsogo Group, 64
Tsɔgɔ (B.31), 64

Wumbu. See Wumu
Wumbvu (B.24), 59
Wumu (B.76), 77
Wuri. See Ɔli

Yaa (B.77c), 77
Yaka. See Yaa
Yambasa (A.62), 36
Yangafɔk (A.72d), 40
Yans (B.85), 81
Yanzi. See Yans
Yasa (A.33), 24
Yaunde. See Ewɔndɔ
Yaunde-Fang Group, 40

For Product Safety Concerns and Information please contact our EU
representative GPSR@taylorandfrancis.com
Taylor & Francis Verlag GmbH, Kaufingerstraße 24, 80331 München, Germany

www.ingramcontent.com/pod-product-compliance
Lightning Source LLC
Chambersburg PA
CBHW052134300426
44116CB00010B/1902